GERONTOLOGY

THE BASICS

Human aging is a complex, multifaceted experience that unfolds over an entire lifetime. While human aging is universal, it is also wildly variable, shaped by individual, social, cultural, political, geographic and historical contexts. *Gerontology: The Basics* explores the field of research, education and practice which takes on the complex and multifaceted questions, issues and problems of adult aging and old age.

Intended for anyone interested in understanding the origins of Gerontology and its unique purview, we invite the reader to join us in a critical examination of what we think we know about becoming and being old and, perhaps, be inspired to engage more deeply in their own travels through the life-course.

Jennifer R. Sasser, Ph.D. is an Educational Gerontologist, transdisciplinary scholar, and community activist. Jenny served as Chair of the Department of Human Sciences and Founding Director of Gerontology at Marylhurst University, in Portland, Oregon, from 1999 to 2015. In 2016, Jenny joined the part-time faculty in the Gerontology program at Portland Community College.

Harry R. Moody, Ph.D. is retired Vice President of Academic Affairs for AARP. DC. He is currently Visiting Professor at Tohoku University in Japan, and Distinguished Visiting Scholar at Fielding Graduate University. He previously served as Executive Director of the Brookdale Centre on Aging at Hunter College and Chairman of the Board of Elderhostel (now Road Scholar).

THE BASICS

For a full list of titles in this series, please visit www.routledge.com/
The-Basics/book-series/B

First published 2018
by Routledge
2 Park Square, Milton Park, Abingdon, Oxon OX14 4RN

and by Routledge
711 Third Avenue, New York, NY 10017

Routledge is an imprint of the Taylor & Francis Group, an informa business

British Library Cataloguing-in-Publication Data
A catalogue record for this book is available from the British Library

Library of Congress Cataloging-in-Publication Data
A catalog record for this book has been requested

ISBN: 978-1-138-77581-7 (hbk)
ISBN: 978-1-138-77582-4 (pbk)
ISBN: 978-1-351-11323-6 (ebk)

Typeset in Bembo
by Sunrise Setting Ltd, Brixham, UK

GERONTOLOGY

THE BASICS

JENNIFER R. SASSER AND HARRY R. MOODY

Routledge
Taylor & Francis Group

LONDON AND NEW YORK

To my daughter Isobel M. Coen as you embark upon adulthood in these wild times. J.R.S.
To Analie Nur, our granddaughter, whose longevity could well reach into the 22nd century. H.R.M.

CONTENTS

LIST OF FIGURES

LIST OF IMAGES

ACKNOWLEDGMENTS

Thank you to the many persons of all ages and life-course stages who have inspired my curiosity about being a human being traveling through the life-course. J.R.S.

My acknowledgment goes out to two people, now deceased, who taught me about aging: Prof. Rose Dobrof, founding Director of the Brookdale Center on Aging at Hunter College, and Laurence Morris, who lived with our family until age 97. H.R.M.

NOTES ON THE AUTHORS

Jennifer (Jenny) R. Sasser, Ph.D. is an Educational Gerontologist, transdisciplinary scholar, and community activist. Jenny has been working in the field of Gerontology for more than half her life, beginning as a nursing assistant and senior citizen advocate before focusing on scholarly inquiry and education. As an undergraduate she attended Willamette University, in Salem, Oregon, graduating Cum Laude in Psychology and Music; her interdisciplinary graduate studies at University of Oregon and Oregon State University focused on the Human Sciences, with specialization areas in adult development and aging, women's studies, and critical social theory and alternative research methodologies. Jenny's dissertation became part of a book published by Routledge in 1996 and co-authored with Dr. Janet Lee – *Blood Stories: Menarche and the Politics of the Female Body in Contemporary US Society*.

For the past twenty years, she has focused her inquiry in the areas of creativity in later life; aging and embodiment; transdisciplinary curriculum design; Critical Gerontological Theory; transformational adult learning practices; and cross-generational collaborative inquiry. Jenny served as Chair of the Department of Human Sciences and Founding Director of Gerontology at Marylhurst University, in Portland, Oregon, from 1999 to 2015.

In 2016, Jenny joined the part-time faculty in the Gerontology program at Portland Community College. Her other commitments include co-authoring *Aging: Concepts and Controversies* (with Harry R. Moody); convening the Gero-Punk Project; serving as a conversation facilitator for Oregon Humanities; and offering consulting, workshops and presentations.

Harry R. Moody, Ph.D. is retired Vice President of Academic Affairs for AARP. DC. He is currently Visiting Professor at Tohoku University in Japan, and Distinguished Visiting Scholar at Fielding Graduate University. He previously served as Executive Director of the Brookdale Center on Aging at Hunter College and Chairman of the Board of Elderhostel (now Road Scholar).

Moody is the author of over 100 scholarly articles, as well as a number of books including: *Abundance of Life: Human Development Policies for an Aging Society* (Columbia University Press, 1988); *Ethics in an Aging* Society (Johns Hopkins University Press, 1992); and co-author of *Aging: Concepts and Controversies*, a Gerontology textbook (co-authored with Jennifer Sasser) now in its 9th edition. His book, *The Five Stages of the Soul*, was published by Doubleday Anchor Books and has been translated into seven languages worldwide.

PREFACE

Aging is everywhere . . . and nowhere! Aging is all around us, but it is also hidden in plain sight. Aging is "everywhere" and "all around us" in that not a day goes by when you don't see a mention made in the media about the benefits of a particular diet for longevity ("Eat this way and live forever!"); or about the multitude of losses that accompany aging and later life – everything from financial resources, to relationships, to social roles, to our very minds; or that "Aging is all in your mind," "Age is just a number," and "You are only as old as you feel."

And, aging is "nowhere" and "hidden in plain sight" in that while there seem to be numerous, often contradictory messages about aging to which we are exposed countless times a day, and while humans seem to be living longer *and* there are more and more older persons around, aging is often assumed to be something that happens to other people, an inevitability that we will have to face at some future point in our own lives, but not something we necessarily choose to contemplate, let alone discuss in our present lives. Nor do most of us consider aging as an experience we are already living.

There are so many mixed messages about aging: Aging is to be embraced; aging is to be avoided. Paradoxically, it seems like many people have discovered aging and are talking about aging, specifically adult aging – mostly how to slow it down and avoid it – but rarely is aging treated in such a way as to offer a balanced portrayal of the personal lifelong human journey of aging nor of aging in adulthood. Is it any wonder that aging and the field of study and practice devoted to understanding it, Gerontology, is often met with confusion, if not entirely ignored?

The truth is, everyone is aging. *You* are aging and you may not have even known it!

In *Gerontology: The Basics*, we hope to offer you a way into exploring not only the field of Gerontology, but also the human experience at the center of this field – the aging journey. What's more, we hope to convince you that there's value in thinking about your own aging journey, and to connecting what we will be discussing in this book with your own experiences, as well as the experiences of others. We aim to show you that aging isn't something that happens only some time later in the life-course but is a lifelong process, nor are old people strange "others" but are our friends, kin and future selves. Even if your own old age seems to be in the distant future there is much you might wish to ponder as you travel through your own life-course. We hope that what we discuss in this book will be helpful to you as you navigate your own and others' aging journeys.

There's a lot of confusion around what Gerontology is. Even highly trained professionals, working in the field of Gerontology, have been known to offer contradictory descriptions of Gerontology, so don't feel badly if you aren't quite sure what it is! That is, in fact, what we'll be exploring throughout this book: What Gerontology is, and isn't; its historical origins and how it constitutes itself as a field of study and practice; and its central ways of constructing knowledge. As well, we'll look closely at the major categories of classic and current research and theory regarding adult aging: the body (biophysical aspects of aging); the mind (psychological aspects of aging); the social (sociological aspects of aging); the political economy of aging; and, perhaps most importantly, the personal meaning(s) of aging, old age and later life.

We are convinced (and we hope to convince you, too) that there is great value in understanding how knowledge about aging is constructed and used, especially the ways in which such knowledge is socially constructed and historically contingent. That is, what we *think we know* about adult aging, later life and old age is not universal nor static, but depends on the social, cultural, political, geographic and historical contexts in which it is produced. Aging is not the same today as it was in the past, nor will it be the same in the future as it is today. As well, as you'll see in subsequent discussions throughout this book, there are enormous variations in how adult aging unfolds and is experienced. So, rather than there being An Aging Experience, there are – surprise! – as many aging experiences as there are individuals traveling through the life-course and into old age. In parallel, you will discover that there are as many different "flavors" of Gerontology as there are Gerontologists focusing their attention on adult development and aging issues. One of our main aims in this book is to explore the question of what holds Gerontology together as a coherent field, given that it contains a multitude of perspectives and practices.

Note to the reader: We want to acknowledge that while we wrote *Gerontology: The Basics* with a general, broad, and potentially international audience in mind, we also wrote from a particular standpoint. We are American Gerontologists who share a certain philosophical worldview, and though we represent different generations of Gerontologists and have experienced different pathways through the field, we both came up in the field of Gerontology, which emerged historically in a predominantly North America and Western European context, during the early decades of its formation and institutionalization. As such, our perspectives on the foundational ideas discussed in this book will be shaped, for better and for worse, by our own experiences of becoming Gerontologists and working for decades in various aspects of the field (as well, we might add, by our own lived experiences as aging persons). At the same time, adult aging is a universal human experience, and population aging and human longevity are increasingly international, global phenomena. In fact, there's an emerging and expanding international gerontological community as well as geographically specific gerontological activities taking place. But, alas, as much as we would have liked to represent these various activities, especially those taking place in non-Western contexts, we weren't able to do so given the scope of this book. What we offer you is a rather high-level, foundational portrayal of Gerontology grounded in our own personal and professional pre-occupations with the field of Gerontology and, more fundamentally, the human aging journey.

Jennifer R. Sasser and Harry R. Moody

INTRODUCTION TO THE FIELD
OF GERONTOLOGY

Time for a short quiz.
  Gerontology is:

1. The scientific study of rocks and minerals.
2. That cool new pop band from France.
3. The study of family lineage and history.
4. The medical speciality that addresses the diseases of aging and later life.
5. None of the above.
6. All of the above.

(The answer: None of the above)

Given the name of this book, *Gerontology: The Basics*, you, the reader, probably assume that we, the authors, have a straightforward, definitive description of Gerontology to offer you. Alas, we don't. As you'll soon discover, there are almost as many definitions of Gerontology as there are people working within the field. Add to that the definitions of people working outside of the field but interested in some of the same questions, issues and problems related to adult aging about which Gerontologists are preoccupied, and the situation gets rather complicated, even confusing. However, when you think about the complex nature of the phenomena upon which Gerontology focuses – the multifaceted aspects of the human aging journey – it makes a certain kind of sense that "Gerontology" means many different things to many different people.

For starters, let's be upfront about what Gerontology is *not*, as that's an easier task than describing what Gerontology *is*. Gerontology is not the same thing as Geriatrics, though they are often mistaken for one another. **Geriatrics** is the medical speciality that focuses on the diseases and disabilities associated with aging and later life, as well as the health and long-term care needs of older adults. Geriatric medicine is an area of training and expertise chosen by some physicians and nurses, though you might come across Geriatric Social Workers as well. Professionals working in Geriatrics hold in common a concern with the special healthcare needs of older adults and the prevention, treatment and management of the diseases and disabilities *associated with* (but not necessarily caused by) adult aging and old age, most commonly heart disease, certain cancers, stroke, Alzheimer's Disease, osteoporosis, arthritis, diabetes, and hypertension. Gerontologists are concerned with these issues as well, but as you'll discover as we venture deeper into our exploration of what constitutes the field of Gerontology, the way Gerontologists think about these and other adult aging issues is quite distinct from how these issues are taken on in Geriatrics. One of the questions we'll pursue in this book is: How do Gerontologists think about and address human aging?

Gerontology, on the other hand, is commonly defined as the scientific study of aging and old age. The term "Gerontology" is attributed to Metchnikoff, who first started using it in 1903. (Interestingly, it was a few years later when Nascher offered the term "Geriatrics" to designate the medical speciality concerned with aging issues.) However, this definition of Gerontology, while pithy and straightforward, belies the complexity of the field. Here are a few of the kinds of descriptions you might come across were you to attempt to suss a definition of Gerontology:

• Gerontology is both a professional practice and an academic discipline that focuses on issues and problems of old age.

- Gerontology is the scientific study of aging, old age and later life.
- Gerontology is an area of healthcare that focuses on the needs of older persons.
- Gerontology is a **multidisciplinary** field that includes perspectives on aging borrowed from other disciplines and professions, such as biology, psychology, sociology, epidemiology, public policy, nursing and social work.
- Gerontology is an **interdisciplinary** enterprise involving the integration of research, theory, and practice from across multiple disciplines.
- Gerontology is only in part a scientific endeavor; Gerontology also includes perspectives from the arts and humanities in order to more deeply understand the lived experience of aging and old age.

We've just scratched the surface. But let us just say that there are multiple, often contradictory – even highly contested – ideas regarding what constitutes Gerontology. Another way into this question is to take a look at the complex and multifaceted phenomenon upon which Gerontologists focus: human aging in adulthood.

FOCUS ON ADULT AGING, LATER LIFE, AND OLD AGE

While human beings – and all living organisms – begin aging from the moment they come into existence, and while Gerontology acknowledges aging as a **life-course** experience, Gerontology focuses primarily on the issues of adult aging, later life, and old age. But there are some important questions we need to ask before we can even land upon a provisional definition of these terms. For starters, what do we mean by "**adult aging**"? If aging is a condition of living, what distinguishes aging in adulthood from aging at other points in the life-course? A related set of questions has to do with the origins of and markers for "**later life**" – a stage in the life-course – and "**old age**," an individual and social status. Put another way, when does adult aging begin, when do we become an "old person," and when does one enter "later life"?

So, those are some important questions we might want to ask about the focus of Gerontology. We'll be saying more – a lot more – about that later. But there are parallel questions we might ask about the people who are doing the work of Gerontology: **Gerontologists**.

What do Gerontologists think they are doing when they are doing Gerontology? What makes Gerontology different from other academic disciplines and fields of study and practice? (That is, in what essential ways is Gerontology distinct from other related disciplines and fields, such as Geriatrics, psychology, sociology, social work, etc.?) How do we know Gerontology is being done when we see it? What are the questions, issues, and problems around which Gerontology organizes and institutionalizes itself? How are these questions, issues, and problems quintessentially gerontological rather than something else? How do you know a Gerontologist when you "see" one?

Here are some of the questions, issues, and problems that preoccupy Gerontologists:

- Gerontologists seek explanations for the causes of aging. Specifically, in Gerontology we want to understand what changes happen to *all* members of the human species, no matter what, as a consequence of the aging process. These changes are often referred to as "**normal aging**" and "**intrinsic aging**." As human beings travel through the life-course and grow older, what changes can be expected to occur as a result of normal, intrinsic aging processes, regardless of the historical, social and cultural contexts in which persons are aging?

- Gerontologists want to be able to tease apart "normal aging" processes from diseases associated with growing older as well as from the effects of living in a particular environment or engaging in particular lifestyles and activities. For example, is it a normal part of the aging process to develop heart disease, or is heart disease correlated with (or associated with) particular lifestyle habits and genetic predispositions which have a cumulative negative effect over time and are, thus, associated with advancing age?

- Gerontologists pursue explanations for how aging processes play out in multiple domains of human experience: body, mind, social world, political economy, and spirit. As well, we wish to understand how aging experiences are both shared and vary between individuals and across individuals living in different historical times, geographic contexts and social spaces.

- Gerontologists seek a deeper, richer understanding of how individuals embody, engage, interpret and narrate the complexities and contradictions of their lived experiences of growing older in particular times, places and spaces.

- Gerontologists are also concerned with how to improve the lives of older adults through political processes, social and economic policies, and community-based programs and services. In other words, creating new knowledge about adult aging, later life and old age isn't enough, Gerontologists want to apply this knowledge in the here-and-now in positive, meaningful ways to improve the quality of life and promote the well-being of persons as they age within their families, communities and societies.

I (Jennifer) was having a conversation with a colleague who directs an undergraduate Gerontology program at a large university in the US about the struggles within the field to articulate a shared definition of what constitutes the field. We agreed that it is difficult to make the case about why Gerontology is an important educational and professional focus when the very people who are responsible for producing and disseminating gerontological knowledge are confused about the nature of the field and how best to talk about it. If we don't have a shared understanding, if not agreement, about what it is we do and why we do it, then how can we expect to continue to nurture and grow the field, as well as communicate with people outside of the field, about what Gerontology is and why it is a worthy and important pursuit? The colleague suggested that perhaps we can understand something about the historical origins and ongoing development of Gerontology by comparing it to a more well-established and well-known discipline: psychology. But I wasn't so sure that this was the approach to take, though analogies can have heuristic value, serving to highlight not only similarities between things, but their differences as well.

Psychology, like Gerontology, considers itself fundamentally to be a scientific discipline in that there is a commitment to basing the body of psychological knowledge on empirical evidence. While psychology has an organizing and shared focus – the individual level of analysis – it is composed of multiple theoretical frameworks, methodological approaches, and foci for inquiry and practice. What holds the diversity of approaches within psychology together, what gives psychology coherence, is the focus on the individual unit of analysis. Of course, the social, cultural, political and historical contexts in which individuals are situated, as well as the influence of biology, are all important factors in psychological research and practice, but they make up the background; in the foreground is the individual and their emotional, intellectual, and behavioral experiences. So far, so good. But what happens when we extend what we know about psychology as a discipline and use it as a template for describing Gerontology?

What Gerontology is and how aging and later life are constructed have much to do with where one stands in terms of their involvement in the field, to such an extent that the outside viewer paying attention may find it difficult reconciling the different problematizations of aging and being an older person. For example, in senior citizen advocacy in the US there's a history many decades' long of fighting for the rights of older adults as if the status of being an older adult was, in and of itself, a minority status and that most older individuals are disadvantaged in some way, necessitating political intervention. As another example, Gerontologists working in community-based social service settings, such as social workers and case managers, often address the needs of older adults who are struggling with chronic physical and mental health issues, economic hardship, and other challenges that aren't necessarily aging issues but which create the causes and conditions for a later life of difficulty.

Given the disparate definitions of Gerontology, and given the complex multifaceted nature of the phenomena at the center of gerontological work, it may be more accurate to describe Gerontology as a professional field that includes practitioners, researchers, educators, policy makers etc. coming from different disciplinary traditions all of whom are committed to understanding, explaining and addressing issues related to adult aging, later life and old age. There are, as such, several related (even nested) dimensions upon which one might describe gerontological work: The disciplinary background from which the individual Gerontologist comes (which has much to do with their education and training – their socialization process into the field – as it does the gerontological "niche" in which they work); within their disciplinary background, the theoretical and/or philosophical commitments that shape how they see the aging phenomena at the center of their work; the context of the work they do as a Gerontologist – are they a researcher, an educator, a policy maker, a service provider? That is, is the work they do primarily about the construction and dissemination of knowledge about aging phenomena from a gerontological perspective – research, theory, and teaching – or about the application of that knowledge in the context of practice? And then there is the specific aging phenomenon or set of phenomena that a particular Gerontologist is interested in understanding more deeply and perhaps developing an explanation for and, hopefully, addressing in some way.

For example, Jennifer's educational preparation for the field of Gerontology included an undergraduate major in psychology and music, and graduate work in multiple Human Sciences disciplines and areas of study: lifespan developmental psychology; critical sociology and anthropology; women's studies; and Gerontology. While she engaged in applied internships and paid work throughout her undergraduate and graduate education in the areas of long-term care, social services, rural health care, and senior citizen advocacy, her primary focus educationally and then professionally has been on educational Gerontology – creating and teaching in educational programs and courses focused on the field of Gerontology for both higher education and community settings. Her scholarly work has been on a parallel track, focusing not on scientific research on aging issues but, rather, on the meanings individuals and collectives make of their experiences traveling through the life-course. She specializes in cross-generational interdisciplinary collaborative inquiry, writing and community-based teaching and learning which focuses on questions about what it means to be a human, including what it means to grow older and experience the last phase of one's life-course.

By comparison and in contrast is Jennifer's colleague A. who focused her educational training at every level on the psychology of aging, specifically on cognitive aging and dementia. A. considers herself to be a "Gero-Psychologist" and works in private practice in the community. She specializes in cognitive assessment for older adults and helps them and their families make decisions about medical and long-term care related to the unique and challenging journey of Alzheimer's Disease. She doesn't conduct research and her primary professional affiliation is as part of the psychological community, and only as an ally to the gerontological community. Yet the work she does is a necessary and important piece of the overall gerontological landscape.

For yet another example, consider L., who doesn't have any educational training in Gerontology but has worked in long-term care settings for several years. The focus of his job is to support the leisure and educational programming of an assisted living community – lifelong learning opportunities, tours, and special events. He interacts with older adults every day and, thus, considers himself to be a Gerontologist.

What do these three professional paths in the field of Gerontology have in common? They each focus in one way or another on issues of aging, later life and old age. But the educational background, specific professional context, and particular focus of each path is very distinct, if not unrelated except for the shared focus on aging phenomena in some fashion. In actual fact, there isn't agreement about what the baseline educational and professional requirements are for being a Gerontologist, though there is an effort in the US, spearheaded by the Association for Gerontology in Higher Education, to establish criteria for Gerontology programs and standardize Gerontology curricula. But in the absence of a unifying paradigm for the field of Gerontology, upon what set of criteria would such standards be predicated?

So, we might ask: What does the world look like through the eyes of a Gerontologist? Do Gerontologists even have enough in common to answer this question? Is there a unitary gerontological lens or, rather, a kaleidoscope composed of multiple lenses? Ferraro, and Neugarten before him, suggests that there is a "gerontological imagination" that might serve as a unifying framework for the gerontological community. We might ask: What are the characteristics of this quintessentially "gerontological imagination," and who is considered to be a member of this community?

IS GERONTOLOGY "MULTIDISCIPLINARY" OR "INTERDISCIPLINARY" (AND DOES IT MATTER?)

"Gerontology" is often referred to as "multidisciplinary" or "inter-disciplinary" in its construction and practice given that the human aging journey is a biophysical, psychological, emotional, and spiritual experience, which is embedded in particular historical, political, economic, and social-cultural contexts. However, these terms are not interchangeable but, rather, indicate different approaches to studying aging issues. "Multidisciplinary" indicates that the study of aging uses multiple perspectives that come from different disciplines – psychology, sociology, political economy, medicine, etc. in a complementary and additive way – aging is complex and multifaceted, and so we must look through different disciplinary lenses to understand aging. In contrast, "interdisciplinary," when used to describe Gerontology, is meant to signify that rather than just adding different perspectives together, these different perspectives are combined or integrated: the sum is greater than its parts. Claims of multidisciplinarity; claims of interdisciplinarity; claims of being a scientific enterprise. It depends upon the level of analysis at which a Gerontologist is working and it depends on the aim of the Gerontologist's work. It depends not only on the location of one's work as a Gerontologist – educational setting, primarily teaching; conducting research; creating and implementing policy; or serving older persons in an applied setting within the community – but also which domain of aging one is focused upon.

Another important question to ask about the work of a Gerontologist is what their view of aging is – do they hold a theoretical framework about adult aging in the context of which they do their work? We'd assert that, based on our long, combined experience in the field, there are many different frameworks operating simultaneously, and not one overarching, unifying approach in Gerontology, despite the notion of a shared "gerontological imagination." As such, one might wonder: If Gerontology is such a multifaceted, distributed field that utilizes and crosses multiple disciplinary boundaries, what do Gerontologists have in common? Is a shared interest in understanding adult aging processes, later life, and the experience of old age enough to hold together the field of Gerontology (especially

if there are multiple, sometimes conflicting, ideas about aging operating simultaneously)? Gerontology is informed by many disciplines
and fields of study, but what might be said about its unique mission?
The dominant "identity" of the field is asserted to be scientific, that
is, focused on accumulating knowledge over time about "law-like"
patterns of human aging, which requires utilizing the perspectives
and processes of scientific inquiry. But Gerontologists are interested
in universal, generalizable explanations as well as understanding the
lived experiences of diverse individuals, as aging is something that
happens to individuals and how individuals make meaning of their
travels through the life-course is fundamentally important.

Perhaps what differentiates Gerontology from related disciplines
and fields of study is that the focus of Gerontology − the "unit of
analysis" − is the holistic, ecological, universal phenomenon of aging
which is mediated by ". . . economic, structural and cultural factors"
(Hendricks et al., 1999, p. 22). Nested within Gerontology are various disciplinary-based, specialized focuses, and within each of these
is a plurality of theoretical, methodological and practice approaches.
You can find people in just about every academic discipline and
field of study and practice who focus their work on aging issues. For
example, there are Psychologists whose research concerns the cognitive changes associated with adult development and aging, sociologists who prioritize how age functions as an organizing principle
in different societal contexts, and political scientists who track the
voting patterns of persons over 65. Other examples can be found
outside the Human Sciences, particularly in cultural studies, ethics
and literature, where there are notable examples of scholars whose
work coalesces around questions about the meaning of aging and
old age at the individual and cultural level. The fact that scholars
and practitioners working in such a wide variety of disciplinary
contexts organize their work around questions about aging, later
life and old age is testament to the persistence and significance of
these questions, as well as their relevance across many disciplines
and fields.

So, we not only need to concern ourselves with the overall focus
of Gerontology as a multifaceted field of inquiry and practice, but
also consider the facet of adult aging − the unit or level of analysis − a
particular Gerontologist is focusing on. Just as the Human Sciences

disciplines can be described according to the unit or level of analysis they focus on – in the case of psychology, the individual unit or level, in the case of sociology, the social group or societal level – we can see that Gerontologists tend to focus their work within a specific unit or level. (The contrary case is the interdisciplinary or transdisciplinary Gerontologist who intentionally integrates perspectives from multiple disciplines and fields, foregrounding a complex question or problem that demands an integrative response. In the case of this kind of work, it is the complexity itself that becomes the "unit of analysis.")

GERONTOLOGICAL RESEARCH AND THEORY

For the most part, Gerontologists are concerned with describing, understanding and explaining multifaceted, interconnected aging phenomena so as to both accumulate knowledge and address what are considered to be the "problems of aging." There are two primary ways that they engage in the ongoing, cumulative process of creating gerontological knowledge: through empirical research and through theory work. We will discuss this with greater depth and detail later in the book, because the preponderance of what is considered to be gerontological knowledge is generated through ongoing research and theory-building. As you will come to discover, there are dominant as well as alternative approaches to both creating new knowledge about aging phenomena through empirical research, as well as creating explanations for aging phenomena through theory-building.

Bengtson, Rice and Johnson, writing in the late 1990s, offered a schema for categorizing the general sets of problems for Gerontologists as they attempt to analyze and understand the multifaceted and interconnected phenomena of aging. This schema continues to have heuristic relevance, especially as the field of Gerontology has grown more complex as it has developed over the past several decades in North America and Western Europe, and more recently internationally. Bengtson et al. suggest that there are three broad categories into which the wide variety of aging phenomena can be organized, at three different levels of analysis: the population level; the social/societal level; and the individual level.

The aged population: This category includes questions and problems regarding members of any population of living organisms which can be considered old because of the length of time they've already lived – their chronological age – as well as how much longer they can be expected to live, or "period life expectancy," based on population mortality data. Bengtson et al. point out that the preponderance of extant gerontological research falls into this category, focusing on the connections between **chronological age** and **functional age**. It is important to emphasize the level of analysis of this category – groups or populations of individuals considered to be old, not the individuals themselves.

The study of age as a social structure: *(Note: this category is listed as the third category in the original discussion; we place it second in order to emphasize the logical progression of levels of analyses, from the population, to the social, to the individual)*: This category includes issues and problems at the center of empirical and theoretical work in Gerontology which focuses on how age functions as an organizing principle of the social world. For example, looking through a sociological lens, a Gerontologist might focus her work on the roles and responsibilities associated with the social status of being an "older adult," or might examine the connections between social institutions that address later life issues, such as long-term care, and the expectations of older adults for what later life might look like. While not called out in the original discussion, fundamentally this level of analysis has to do with the **socially constructed meanings** given to particular chronological ages and life-course stages, and is a bridging category in that it attends to the ways in which individual meanings of, expectations about, and behaviors related to age and aging are shaped by social structures and discourses.

Aging as a developmental process: Whereas the first category focuses on the population level, this category includes questions regarding how individual members of a species, in this case the human species, experience the lifelong process of development, growth and aging. Work in this category may focus on the psychological, social or biological dimensions of aging as a time-dependent, emergent phenomenon. Examples of gerontological work that fits into this category include **longitudinal research** that follows a group of people, asking them the same set of questions at different points in time about some aspects of their experience as they move through the life-course. By following the same people over decades, researchers can track what changes, what stays the same, how individuals' experiences vary or don't. Notable examples of this kind of research include the Harvard Men's Study; the Seattle Longitudinal Study; and the Irish Longitudinal Study on Aging. As well, contextual factors that may shape the specific aging experiences being examined can be considered as part of the study, rather than controlled, as is the case in the more typical **cross-sectional research** study in which different groups which vary only in terms of chronological age are compared at one point in time.

We can't emphasize enough the "nested," embedded nature of the levels of analyses represented by these three conceptual categories of aging phenomena. The population level is composed of individuals, and both individuals and groups of individuals dwell within the social world, a world full of meanings simultaneously constructed and contested in the process of traveling through one's life-course as a social being whose life is embedded in a particular historical time and social, cultural and political contexts. The challenge for Gerontologists, whatever their disciplinary and professional focus happens to be, is to account for the inherent complexity of aging phenomena, on the one hand, while attempting to manage this complexity by disentangling these "mutually dependent phenomena," on the other hand. This is such an important key to understanding the gerontological "thought space" – and the source of both its inherent challenges and, for those of us working in Gerontology, sustained fascination – that you'll see this motif appearing again.

SOCIAL GERONTOLOGY AND THE LIFE-COURSE PERSPECTIVE

Underneath the large tent of Gerontology is the sub-area of Social Gerontology. The early development of North American Gerontology in the 20th century was closely aligned to Geriatrics and focused primarily on the problems of aging and old age associated with physical decline, infirmity and vulnerability. Early social welfare programs in Europe and North America were predicated on the construction of old age as a time of loss and vulnerability, and the idea that society held some responsibility for ensuring the well-being of its older citizens. Starting in the late 19th century and into the early 20th century, chronological age became a standardized marker for particular life-course stages and as a criterion for eligibility for social and economic programs geared toward the "elderly."

Social Gerontology focuses on the intersection between aging persons, who are more than just their aging bodies, and social structures. The aging human at the center of social gerontological research and practice is a complex **bio-psycho-social** being whose life unfolds in specific social, cultural, economic, political, environmental and historical contexts. Mostly what Social Gerontology does is describe aging-related patterns and development over time, not the underlying, universal mechanisms of aging. Rather than focusing on the biophysical aging changes that may occur in human (and other) organisms, Social Gerontologists are concerned with *how* these changes are embedded in and shaped by larger systems, and the ways in which humans engage in the multifaceted aging process and experience later life in different times, places, and spaces. For example, of interest might be the way in which physical environments can either support or undermine an individual's ability to function as independently as possible in later life, or how behavioral interventions and modifications may stave off or ameliorate negative health outcomes associated with growing older but not caused by biological aging itself. As another example, the lived experiences of LGBTQ older adults living in heteronormative assisted living facilities may be the focus of inquiry, with the ultimate outcome being the development of "best practices" around serving diverse communities of older persons.

At the heart of Social Gerontology is the **Life-Course Perspective**. This perspective foregrounds aging as a lifelong process that unfolds from infancy through the farthest reaches of old age. As such, aging isn't something that begins at some arbitrary point later in the adult life-course, nor is old age disconnected from all the other stages that an individual has passed through previously. Instead, aging is seen as a multifaceted (bio-psycho-social) and contextualized process intertwined with development throughout the entire span of a human being's time on earth. From the life-course perspective, who one is and the experiences – both normative and non-normative – one has had at every life-course stage are consequential for their experience of old age. However, it is important to note that, while many Gerontologists working in Social Gerontology and the field more broadly acknowledge that aging is a lifelong process, most gerontological work – research, education and practice – focuses on the adult aging process and issues of later life and old age. Stay-tuned, as later in this book, you'll see how the life-course perspective is employed in the context of research on the social and political economy aspects of adult aging.

Intermission: Age is strange

One of the ways we track where we are in our own travels through the life-course is by noting where our close ones are in *their* travels through the life-course. The occasion of celebrating the birthday of a dear, close other, whatever species they happen to be a member of, offers one a moment of pause, an opportunity to reflect upon how it is that our precious lives are so tangled up together.

+++

I just slid into the oven a sheet of coconut macaroons flecked with bittersweet chocolate. Macaroons – the down-to-earth flaked coconut haystack kind, not the fancy French bonbon kind (though both are equally delicious!) – are my mother's favorite cookie. I gave her a big mason jar full of them (a total of 12) as one of her Christmas presents. Purportedly, she allows herself to eat one a day, so by my calculations, if she began consuming them on December 25th she ran out of her macaroon supply around January 5th (give or take a day or two on either side of January 5th, in case she ate more than one macaroon on a particular day or, perhaps, skipped a day). So, time for me to replenish her supply!

The day I write this is my mother's 70th birthday. The macaroons are one of the gifts I am giving her.

During our texting conversation this morning, when I wished her a happy birthday, she asked, "Am I really 70?!?! How did that happen?"

My response: "Age is strange."

Age (and aging) *is* strange.

Where does "70" reside? (Or "7" or "17"?)

Certainly, after having lived on this planet, with its gravity and other peculiar forces, for several decades, one's body shows and feels the impact. But what does "70" look like. Where does "70," or any age, reside?

+++

The accumulation of birthdays is probably the least informative and interesting definition of one's "age."

What would happen if, instead, we defined aging as the process of becoming more complex through a life deeply lived? Where would our age reside within such a definition? Rather than our chronological ages, perhaps we'd talk about our lived experiences (especially the messy ones), and what we've learned about ourselves, and others, through ongoing thinking and reflecting (alone and together), and by being willing over and over to try to have delicate, brave conversations.

What if, in addition to noting our own and others' chronological ages, we marked our travels through the life-course by celebrating how long it is that we've been flying together through space and time?

What if we toasted to the shared mystery of embodying a particular age, all ages and no age, all at once?

Perhaps the best question we could ask, upon the occasion of a birthday, would be: How long has it been that we've been loving each other?

From Jennifer Sasser, www.geropunkproject.org

AGING: EVERY BODY'S DOING IT!

What is aging? When does aging begin and what are its underlying causes? When does one become an old person? When does the life-course stage of "later life" commence? What can be said to happen to all members of the human species over the course of a lifetime, regardless of when and where they live and who they are? These are perennial questions central to gerontological inquiry and practice, and we can ask these questions about each of the domains in which aging takes place: the biological, psychological, social, even cultural and political.

The largest body of research both within and outside of Gerontology related to exploring the questions "When does aging begin?" and, "What constitutes the aging process for all members of the human species?" focuses on biological aging. This is not surprising, given the historical connection between Geriatrics and Gerontology, as well as the fact that aging has been seen (and is still seen) as being fundamentally a biological process that originates from within an organism.

Aging is a system of interconnected phenomena

Human aging isn't a single phenomenon but, rather, a system of interconnected phenomena taking place at multiple levels of analysis simultaneously:

Body: genetics; biology; physiology; neurology

Mind: emotion; cognition; personality; attitudes; behaviour; meaning; consciousness

Social: roles and responsibilities, family, friends, community, social systems and institutions

Political economic: political and economic systems and policies

Historical: generations (age cohorts); large-scale events that shape the life-course; zeitgeist

---

Most fundamentally, aging can be said to be a biological process that unfolds over time and that all living creatures experience. Referred to as **senescence**, biological aging begins at conception and continues through the life-course of each member of a species until the time of their death. Aging and dying are not the same processes, though the trajectory of a human life-course is from birth to death, and the normal biological aging process does seem to lead ultimately to the demise of the human body. Nor is aging a disease, though there are chronic diseases that increase in prevalence with increasing age, such as heart disease, diabetes, stroke, dementia and certain kinds of cancers. Let us emphasize that these diseases are not caused by a normal aging process but are *associated* with increasing age, along with other interrelated factors such as gender, ethnicity, social determinants of health, the environments in which one lives, and lifestyle. What's more, there are striking differences in the rate at, and extent to which, the biological changes associated with aging happen at the individual level. But the bottom line is: the changes associated with senescence happen to some extent, at some point, to all human beings.

As we'll explore in the chapter on the aging body, there are several different theories of biological aging, but what they all hold in common is that they describe **intrinsic** processes caused by **endogenous** factors that are true to some extent for all members of a species as they travel through time. By "intrinsic," we mean that these changes originate from within rather than without the organism and by "endogenous," that they are governed by genetically driven processes. These intrinsic, endogenous biological changes, often referred to as **"bio-markers,"** result in decreased reserve capacity and increased vulnerability to functional limitations, accidents, chronic disease and, ultimately, death.

There are also **exogenous** factors **extrinsic** to the human body that influence the process of senescence, such as access to health care and education, clean water and nutritious food, environmental exposure, and "lifestyle" habits. The human body is not a closed system, as recent research on epigenetics has demonstrated; there's a relationship between the inside and the outside to such an extent that it is difficult to tease apart the intrinsic and extrinsic factors in order to determine exactly what causes biological aging. As well, the human body isn't separate from the sociocultural, political and environmental contexts in which it is situated, nor from the individual consciousness that is embodied within the soma. This begs the question: What are the fundamental, normal biological changes that can be said to be caused by aging, in and of itself?

Fundamentally, what scientists who study the biology of aging are seeking is not only a *description* of biological aging that is universally true for all members of the human species despite the historical, cultural, social and environmental contexts in which they live, but an *explanation* as to how and why aging happens and the extent to which the mechanisms and processes responsible for aging are modifiable.

One of the "Big Questions" of Gerontology has to do with the extent to which biological aging processes can be delayed, slowed down, even prevented all together. However, there are several issues that continue to vex those who focus their research on the biological causes of aging. For example, one persistent question has to do with to what extent the biological changes that are thought to occur with increasing age are caused by normal aging processes, as opposed to factors that are correlated or associated with aging but not caused by aging in and of itself. This distinction between "*correlated with*" and "*caused by*" is essential and can't be emphasized enough; just because there are biological changes that have been observed as happening for the majority of humans as they grow older doesn't necessarily mean that these changes are caused by processes intrinsic to aging. (This distinction between "causation" and "correlation" will be taken up again in the context of a more in-depth discussion of methodological approaches used in gerontological research.)

Another challenge to the quest for a universal description of, and explanation for, aging is the significant differences between individuals in terms of the rate at and degree to which they show biological – and other – aging changes. Gerontologists refer to this as **heterogeneity in aging** ("heterogeneity" being a fancy word for "difference"). Despite the common age stereotype that the older we get the more alike we become, in fact, as demonstrated repeatedly in empirical studies on a variety of aging-related changes, individuals become less alike, not more alike, with each passing year. We not only accumulate birthdays with the passing of time, we accumulate life experiences, and these life experiences increase our complexity as human beings. The farther away from the biological level of analysis we go, into the psychological, social, environmental and cultural layers of aging, the less generalizable and universal our descriptions and explanations are. We move from "**nomothetic**" explanations to "**ideographic**" explanations, that is, from the universal level of analysis to the individual level of analysis. And yet, to understand adult aging as deeply as we can, as well as be highly effective when interacting with older persons, we need both kinds of explanations.

THE BODY IS ONLY PART OF THE STORY

Humans are not only biological organisms but embodied minds, members of societies and cultures, and creatures of particular times, places and spaces. What happens to the body as it travels through time on the planet earth is only part of the story, though it is often the part of the story about aging we hear the most about (and is certainly the part of the story that receives the most attention in terms of research and intervention). The story is much more complex, as aging takes place on multiple dimensions simultaneously, and each dimension has its own trajectory and dynamics. Ultimately and fundamentally, aging plays out in the context of an individual's lived experience. And this "lived experience" is influenced and shaped by **social structures**, cultural meanings, and the layers of contexts in which one's life is embedded. As such, the Big Question, What is aging? might be best addressed with yet another question: "For whom?" In the same vein, "What characterizes later life and old age?" might best be responded to with a similar question, "For whom and in what contexts?" Aging is multifaceted, context-dependent and the aging experience itself so wildly varied at the individual level that the search for a nomothetic or universal definition of and explanation for what constitutes aging is elusive, if not impossible. And yet, the "gerontological quest" has changed little since the emergence of Gerontology in the mid-20th century as an organized field of study and practice: To develop theoretical insights informed by empirical research regarding what constitutes "normal aging" for all members of the human species.

As we move from the biological aspects of aging, into the psychological, social and cultural realms, we move from basic scientific explanations into considerations of the meanings given to aging experiences. While Gerontology is often described as a scientific field, and while the preponderance of gerontological researchers are conducting empirical research designed with the purpose of developing law-like explanations for changes associated with aging, the research on the psychological, social and cultural aspects of aging provides insights into patterns of experience and meaning-making for aging and older individuals or groups of older adults, as well as the meanings of aging, old age and later life across cultures.

The hallmark of scientific research methodology is that the phenomenon being examined is decontextualized, any factors that might influence the variables being examined are controlled in some way, in terms of the sampling procedures used to assemble a group of research participants, as well as in terms of how data is collected and analyzed statistically. There are sophisticated methodological designs that allow researchers to isolate significant factors so as to determine the strength and direction of their relationships. But as we've begun to describe, adult aging is a context-dependent, contingent process and to understand how it is experienced requires a different set of theoretical and empirical approaches, approaches that are sensitive to context and foreground meaning at the individual and societal levels.

BUILDING BLOCKS OF GERONTOLOGICAL KNOWLEDGE

As aging is a multifaceted process, unfolding over time across multiple domains, there are multiple definitions of aging. The most common and basic definition is **chronological aging**, or the number of years an individual has lived since the day they were born. This is what most people think of when they think about issues of aging, old age and later life – how many years a person has been alive, how many birthdays they have celebrated (or avoided?). But this doesn't tell us *how* one is aging or experiencing their travels through the lifecourse. To know more, we have to look at each domain in which aging takes place, according to criteria specific to that domain; this is exactly what we'll be doing in later chapters of this book. Before we discuss adult aging in the domains of body, mind, society and political economy – as well as meaning-making in later life – it is important to discuss an issue central to the scientific study of aging, and that is how chronological age functions as a **variable**.

Pause, Reflect, Connect: Where does age reside?

If you didn't know the year of your birth, what age would you say you are?

At its most basic, scientific research examines the relationship between variables. Variables are measureable constructs that are posited to connect to some phenomenon, in this case, the various phenomena associated with adult aging. Further, Gerontologists conducting scientific research on aging processes are interested in **correlations**, or the direction and strength of the relationship between variables. Most typically based on a combination of observation and hypothesizing, a relationship between variables is tested to see if a particular variable (or set of variables) affects another particular variable (or set of variables). The variable hypothesized to exert the effect is called the "**independent variable**," and the variable hypothesized to be affected by the independent variable is referred to as the "**dependent variable**." You might remember much of what we are discussing here from basic science courses – we are talking about the fundamental components of hypothesis testing and scientific experimental design.

Gerontologists want to know what causes aging and what aging causes. But aging doesn't function as a variable in the way that other human constructs function as variables. Aging is a multi-causal phenomenon, that is, it is dependent on many other factors that exist at multiple levels of analysis; as such, as a dependent variable it is caused by or associated with many other potential variables. Nor does it work very well as an independent variable, because aging as a phenomenon isn't independent of context or other factors and thus can't function in any pure sense as a variable that causes other things to happen – as such, chronological age, the number of years one has been on the planet since one's birth, can't function in hypothesis testing as an independent variable because, in and of itself, it doesn't cause any other phenomenon; it is a marker for other things thought to be associated with aging processes, but age in and of itself isn't a causal variable.

This has many implications for the scientific study of aging. If chronological age can't function as an independent variable in hypothesis testing, then how do gerontological researchers determine what is caused by aging and what is associated with aging? At its most basic, chronological age serves as a proxy variable for other phenomena considered to be associated with the multifaceted aging process. That is, researchers studying aging assume that chronological age is *associated with* (or "correlated with"), if not causing, other changes happening at the various levels of the complex human aging system.

FUNCTIONAL AGE

Another conventional way Gerontologists respond to the fundamental complexity of aging phenomena – you'll come across this concept quite frequently in gerontological research as well as in the assessment of how individual older adults are faring – is the idea of **functional age** for segments of the older adult population. Rather than using a singular chronological age, categories of age ranges are used instead: The "**young-old**" group is composed of adults ages 65–74; the "**old-old**" group, ages 75–84; and the "**oldest-old**" group are those persons 85 years of age and older. More recently, a "**centenarian**" segment has been added to reflect increasing longevity and the expansion of the number of persons 100 years of age and older.

What's important to understand about these age groupings is that they aren't only chronological ranges, but are associated with average patterns for, and general descriptions of, how individuals falling within each category *might* be expected to function and the kinds of services they might need. For example, a Gerontologist might wish to determine the extent to which an older person is able to manage independently their **Activities of Daily Living (or ADLs)**: personal care activities such as bathing, dressing, toileting and moving around, as well as instrumental tasks such as cooking, cleaning and other daily chores. In other words, these functional age categories are descriptive *and* proscriptive; Gerontologists use these conventional concepts frequently in research and practice as a way to manage the inherent complexity of, and variability in, the adult aging process, to suss how an individual of a particular age is functioning – their functional age – in relation to their own baseline capacities, as well as in comparison to their age-mates and the normative standards and expectations for the age category into which they fit at any given time.

AGE/PERIOD/COHORT

The **age/period/cohort** triad gets to the heart of the matter when it comes to the ongoing gerontological quest. The issue at question is: When considering a phenomenon that happens in later life and is theoretically associated with adult aging, to what extent is this phenomenon due to normal, universal **aging processes** (remember that chronological age is a stand-in for the aging process itself), to some factor significant during the **period** of time during which the phenomenon is observed or empirically studied, or the result of **cohort differences** or the experiences members of a generation share because of when they were born. Another way to put this is that Gerontologists are trying to disentangle the effects of aging processes ("**age effects**"), experiences a group of people share in common regardless of their ages ("period effects"), and experiences members of an age cohort share in common because of when they were born and traveled through time ("cohort effects").

The Baby Boomer cohort is often held up as the quintessential example of how "cohort effects" can shape the expectations and experiences of an entire generation. Because of when the Baby Boomers were born – post-World War II – and the societal changes that took place during their formative years as children, as well as because of the large size of this cohort cross-nationally, there are aging and later life expectations and experiences they hold in common (there were pronounced post-war "baby booms" in North America, the UK, France, The Netherlands, Denmark, Sweden and Switzerland). The question is, how much of a bearing do these shared cohort experiences have on the aging of the Baby Boomers living in various countries? And what about "period effects," such as the economic downturn that happened in the US and then globally beginning in 2007–2008 or Brexit in the UK in 2017?

Period effects are the effects of large-scale events that all members of society, regardless of age or cohort, experience. However, the influence of a period effect is modified by chronological age and birth cohort – when in history one was born and the age one is when a large-scale event takes place. Such events are often national or global in nature – wars, elections, epidemics, environmental or political crises, the widespread introduction of new technology – though period effects can also be seen more locally, for example when a community experiences a significant positive event like economic recovery or a negative event such as a factory explosion or the discovery of lead in its municipal drinking water. The point here is that most members of a community or society are exposed to the same large-scale historically time-bound event, but they aren't affected in uniform ways. A clear example of this is a situation like a war – all people alive during the time of war are impacted, but a young child is impacted differently than, say, a young adult who could be conscripted into military battle or the parents who will worry about them when they go away to war.

An added layer of complexity that is important to recognize is that an age cohort or generation is composed of many diverse individuals. Age doesn't stand alone, nor is an age cohort monolithic. Rather, our travels through the life-course are influenced and modified by our social statuses – gender and gender identification, ethnicity and race, class, education level and occupational background, cultural background, health status and disability – as well as the social stratification systems connected to these social statuses. As mentioned previously, heterogeneity in aging, not uniformity, is the rule. As we grow older, we become less like our age-mates because of who we are as an individual – body, mind, and spirit in context – and the accumulation over our life-course of both shared ("normative") and unique ("non-normative") life experiences. On a related note, increasing attention is being given in Gerontology to the **social determinants of health** in later life, how individuals' aging experiences are strongly influenced by who they are, where they live, and their access to social and economic resources and capital. This is why, to reiterate, the question of "Aging *for whom?*" is so important to have at the front of one's mind when exploring issues of adult aging. Aging is a universal human experience and, at the end of the day, aging emerges from and unfolds within the context of our individual lives.

Pause, reflect, connect: Age doesn't stand alone

As you reflect upon your sense of self (both how you feel inside and how you present yourself to the world), how important is your current age and life-course stage? How important is your ethnicity, race, and cultural background? How important is your class or educational level? What about your gender and sexual identity? Your religious beliefs? Your political commitments?

How do these different facets combine or intersect in terms of who you are and how you live your life?

Is aging a single phenomenon, or multiple interconnected phenomena that happen in the different domains that compose the human being? Do aging processes originating from within the body abide by the same principles as psychological, social, political–economic, or existential aging processes? The evidence to date, as well as lived human experience, would suggest strongly that there are different processes happening simultaneously at different levels of the human being which might be described as "aging," and that aging unfolds in a multitude of ways across individuals, societies and historical contexts. As such, Gerontology may not be a singularly focused discipline but a multidisciplinary field of inquiry and practice as complex as the phenomena under its purview.

AN "EPIC" STORY: HUMAN LONGEVITY

Gerontology as a distinct field of study and practice quite possibly wouldn't even exist if it weren't for the relatively recent phenomenon in the history of human beings on the planet earth: longevity.

As long as there have been groups of human beings living together, there have been members of the group identified as being longer-lived compared to other members of the group. Of course, just because an individual is the oldest member of their tribe or family or community doesn't mean that they are in fact old, just that they've managed to live longer than anyone else has. This is an important distinction to make, between one's age position within one's social context and one's longevity. For most of human history, humans didn't live much beyond what we now consider to be the beginning of the long stretch of adulthood – the third or perhaps the fourth decade. Whether from intrinsic causes such as illness or disease, or extrinsic causes such as predation or environmental forces, the human life-course was short and intense. To what extent did being relatively long-lived within such a context confer status and power? Sociology tells us that age is one of the statuses that organizes social groups, and that in different historical, social, and cultural contexts, advanced age (which is, as we've pointed out, always relative) is given a variety of different meanings.

But something significant began to happen in the late 19th century in the Western world and by the end of the 20th century, the average life expectancy at birth had increased by 30 years, from approximately 48 to 78 years of age. Let's pause for a moment and wrap our minds around this – in a mere 100 years, human beings living in North America and Western Europe gained on *average* 30 additional years of life – that's a remarkable increase! Because life expectancy (not to be confused with maximum lifespan) measure- ments are statistical averages, it follows that half the population falls on either side of the average, so some individuals within the popu- lation live fewer years than the average, and some individuals within the population live greater years than the average.

Both **life expectancy** and **lifespan** numbers describe trends at the level of a population. Average life expectancy can be measured from birth or any age, and within particular contexts – for different countries, for example – and for different sub-categories of people, such as according to gender or ethnicity. As we'll discuss later in the book, there are staggering disparities in life expectancy among existing birth cohorts on the basis of ethnicity and other social positionalities. For example, while more males than females are conceived, the life expectancy – or "death rate" – for males is higher than for females at every age.

Fundamentally, what a life expectancy statistic tells us is how long on average one might expect to live, starting from a particular age – at birth, or at 65, for example. The major gain in average life expectancy made during the 20th century was in life expectancy from birth – that is, a reduction in death rates at birth and in childhood – rather than a significant elongation of years lived in advanced adulthood. Nonethe- less, one of the stories that can be told about many Western countries is that by the end of the 20th century more people were living longer and older persons composed a larger proportion of the population.

We can also look at life expectancies for people living in other countries, as population aging is happening not only in North America and Western Europe, but globally. Longevity is a global phenom- enon (as can be seen in Figure 1.1) – worldwide, humans are living longer as social conditions change, which means that there is a larger proportion of older persons in the world's population than has ever been true at any other historical time. There are variations in the rate at which this trend plays out country-by-country, but according to demographers who study these trends, there are three major factors

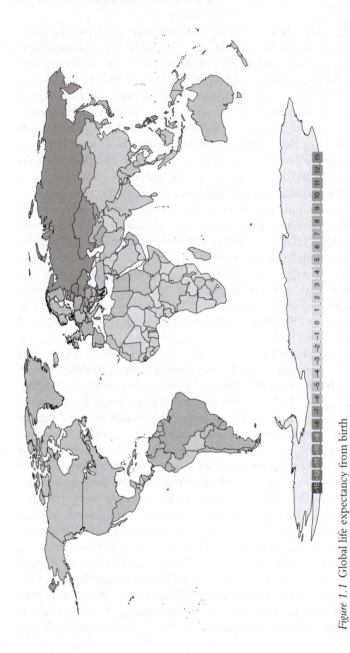

Figure 1.1 Global life expectancy from birth

Credit: By Lpele (Own work) [CC BY-SA 4.0 (https://creativecommons.org/licenses/by-sa/4.0)], via Wikimedia Common.

that contribute to this worldwide trend: decreases in fertility or birth-rate; increases in average life expectancy or longevity; and the related phenomenon of increasing numbers of older adults in various populations as large cohorts move together through time.

Often, life expectancy and lifespan get confused and used inter-changeably. While these are related concepts, they are not the same and it is important when discussing population aging to understand the difference. While both life expectancy and lifespan are measurements that give us a sense of what's happening for populations of humans, they don't tell us much about what any individual might expect. And they have another significant difference: life expectancy takes into account the environmental and social context in which members of a population are aging, whereas lifespan measurements are decontextualized and indicate how long a species, in this case the human species, might be able to live in the absence of influences from the outside, such as injuries and accidents, as well as negative consequences which might be said to originate from within the human, such as serious illness and diseases which shorten one's lifespan potential.

So, back to the "epic" story of increases in human longevity during the 20th century. In the span of a mere one hundred years, the average life expectancy increased by 30 years. An increase of this size, as far as historical and fossil records suggest, is unprecedented. As a result, there are more long-lived people living among us than ever before. At the same time – and this is important to understand – the maximum human lifespan, officially documented at 122 years, hasn't changed. While we've been considering population aging, we might wonder about the significant increase in human longevity – more people living longer – and how this plays out for individuals? Who has benefitted, and who hasn't, from increases in human longevity? And, an important related question: some of us may gain additional years in adulthood, but what is the quality of these additional years? These are some of the "Big Questions" asked in Gerontology.

HOW AGING PROCESSES ARE STUDIED

While Gerontology aspires to be a scientific discipline, this aspiration can be only partially realized because of the very nature of the phenomena at the center of inquiry and practice. The hallmark of scientific research is that it is characterized by hypothesis testing through experimental design in order to develop "objective" descriptions of, and explanations for, universal and law-like principles and patterns. But social gerontological research is first and foremost concerned with how human beings living in particular times, places and spaces experience adult aging, old age and later life. True experimental design requires that a large group of randomly acquired human subjects is assembled (the larger the better for statistical analyses purposes) and that individual subjects are randomly assigned to different groups, each of which receives a different "dose" of the variable in question – a particular kind of behavioral or medical intervention, for example. Researchers conducting true experiments want to determine the extent to which there are statistically significant differences in outcomes for the control group – the group that receives no intervention – and the experimental groups that receive different levels or "doses" of the intervention. Because the sample sizes for experimental research are so large and randomly assembled it is assumed that the sample represents the larger population from which it was obtained. Another very important assumption is that any individual-level differences or characteristics of the research subjects will be evenly distributed across the random sample and, thus, won't get in the way of the variables being examined in the research.

ETHICAL CONSIDERATIONS

You might at this point be wondering about the ethical implications of experimental research with human subjects. There are many issues that need to be considered when conducting any research with human beings, especially when conducting true experiments. For example, it would be unethical to prevent members of the control group from receiving an intervention that could potentially improve their lives; conversely, it would be unethical to expose members of an experimental condition to an intervention that caused harm. Sometimes researchers don't know whether an intervention will be helpful or harmful – that's why, in fact, they are conducting research to begin with! But in the course of conducting their research they may discover that there is such a significant difference between outcomes for the control group compared to the experimental group that they decide to modify or suspend their research. There are recent examples of medical research in which the intervention being experimentally evaluated proved to be so beneficial that the research was suspended and all subjects – for the control group and experimental group alike – were offered the intervention. The opposite situation has been seen as well, experimental research in which it was determined that either the intervention had a neutral effect or that harm was coming to members of the experimental group that was unreasonable and, thus, the research was suspended. On a related side note, recent research on the placebo effect, or the "no treatment condition," offers some provocative insights about the power of "positive thinking"; there is an increasing body of research that demonstrates that a subject's belief that an intervention will have a positive outcome, even in the absence of any intervention, can be enough to produce a statistically significant improvement in outcomes.

While true experimental design isn't possible for most research on adult aging, there are two central methodological designs that are used in social gerontological research: **cross-sectional** and **longitudinal**. Of the two, the cross-sectional design is used in the preponderance of research aiming to develop scientific explanations of aging phenomena, whether caused by aging itself or associated with aging. One way to think about these two research designs is that each one controls or holds steady one of the three effects discussed earlier – age, period or cohort – so that the individual and combined impact of the other two effects can be examined. In cross-sectional research, in which groups of participants of different ages are measured at one point in time and then compared – the comparison groups are of different ages and generations, but each group is composed of people within the same chronological age range and thus represent the same age cohort – but period effects are controlled for because different age/cohort groups are being measured at the same point in time. As well, researchers using the cross-sectional methodological design attempt to control for any other extraneous factors that might get in the way of, or "confound," their ability to suss the relationship between age and the phenomenon they are studying. Examples of such factors are educational level, economic status, health status, gender, ethnicity or professional background. Because the aim of cross-sectional research in Gerontology is to see if there is a statistically significant difference in the average performance of the older subjects compared to the younger subjects that might provide insight into the aging process itself, the groups being compared, which differ according to age and cohort, need to be as similar on other characteristics as possible.

But here's the rub: differences due to aging can't actually be determined by cross-sectional research because what you get is a "snap-shot" of how people of different ages are doing on some measure *at one point in time*. One wonders if differences between the younger and older subjects are due to cohort difference or due to aging differences (either differences caused by aging itself or associated with aging), but there's no way to know if what is being observed or measured in cross-sectional research is an outcome of true aging changes and differences, or because of cohort differences. Gerontologists can learn a great deal from cross-sectional research about how cohort groups differ from each other, or **"between-group differences,"** as well as how individuals *within* a cohort differ from one another, or **"inter-individual differences."** In order to know if a difference *between* age groups or between individuals *within* an age group is due to aging processes or other factors, the same group of individuals must be followed over long stretches of time to see how they develop and change. This is where the other primary methodological approach to gerontological research comes into play.

If the analogy for cross-sectional research is a photograph, the analogy for longitudinal research is film. Longitudinal methodology in the context of Gerontology involves selecting a group of people representing the same age cohort and following them over time to see how they change – or don't – in particular areas.

International Studies & Networks

- Australian Longitudinal Study of Ageing
- Brazilian Longitudinal Study of Ageing and Well Being
- Canadian Longitudinal Study on Aging
- China Health and Retirement Longitudinal Study
- English Longitudinal Study of Ageing

- Health and Retirement Study
- Japanese Study of Aging and Retirement
- Korean Longitudinal Study of Ageing
- Longitudinal Ageing Study in India
- Mexican Health and Aging Study
- Survey of Health, Ageing and Retirement in Europe
- Integrative Analysis of Longitudinal Studies of Aging

What's of interest here are **continuities and discontinuities**, the balance between **gains and losses**, in areas such as physiological functioning and health; psychological characteristics such as behaviors, attitudes, beliefs, mental health and personality traits; and social dimensions such as relationships, family life, living arrangements, work and leisure. Longitudinal research design entails collecting data from the same group of people periodically over a long stretch of time, say, every five or ten years for several decades. This is the only way to keep track of changes over time that might be attributable to intrinsic aging processes, and because the same group of people representing the same age cohort is followed over time, potential cohort effects can be controlled or ruled out. Individuals in the sample are compared to themselves, that is, each participant serves as his or her own "baseline" to which subsequent measures on key variables are compared. As well, individuals within the sample being studied over time are compared to each other, which can offer researchers insights into individual differences or "heterogeneity in aging."

A recent cross-sectional study of a subset of participants from the Irish Longitudinal Study on Aging (TILDA) serves as an interesting case study for many of the conceptual and methodological complexities of empirical research on aging that we've been discussing. The researchers, Robertson and Kenny, wondered whether self-perceptions of aging might *modify* the relationship between two variables: "frailty" and "cognitive function." A "modifying variable" is a variable that can modify the relationship between the Independent

Variable and the Dependent Variable. To dive more deeply, check out their study:

Robertson, D.A., & Kenny, R.A. (2015). Negative Perceptions of Aging Modify the Association Between Frailty and Cognitive Function in Older Adults. *Personality and Individual Differences.*

But as with cross-sectional design, there are some challenges and limitations inherent in longitudinal design, foremost among them that there's no way to know if changes being observed over time are due to intrinsic aging or aging-related processes or due to the time of measurement, or period effects. Other limitations are that longitudinal research requires a great deal of commitment from researchers who are interested in sustaining their attention on a long-term project. As well, longitudinal research is expensive, there's the potential for what are called "practice effects" as the participants are being measured in the same ways repeatedly over time, and there's the problem of attrition – participants may discontinue participating. In fact, over time the size of the sample of participants in longitudinal research reduces in number as participants become unable to participate due to changing life circumstances, infirmity or even death.

The longitudinal and cross-sectional research designs have been the standard approaches for as long as Gerontology has been a field of research, study and practice. There have been more recent innovations in methodological designs and statistical analytic approaches that allow researchers to examine multiple age cohorts over time. Referred to as a **"cross-sequential design,"** this design simultaneously takes into account age effects, period effects, and cohort effects while examining differences and similarities *between* age cohorts, and change and stability over time for individuals. This is a powerful, complicated and not terribly common research methodology used in Gerontology, but important to mention nonetheless.

Idea for further exploration

How do Gerontologists go about trying to disentangle the effects of underlying aging processes from the multitude of potential *aging-related* factors? To offer a concrete example, suppose we wanted to find out if memory loss is an inevitable and normal part of growing older. How might we go about examining this question?

The first place to begin would be to specify more precisely what aspect of memory one was interested in examining for changes with aging – short-term memory for words – a shopping list, perhaps? – or names? Recall of information stored in long-term memory, such as one might have learned in school or at work? Everyday memory for how to go about doing things, such as instructing someone else about how to fix something or make a particular recipe? After determining the kind of memory capacity – or construct – being examined, the next step is to articulate a hypothesis, or statement that describes the relationship between the construct and aging, for example, that memory for everyday tasks improves with increasing age (or, conversely, that short-term memory capacities decline with increasing age). After getting clear about the hypothesis at the centre of the research, one must then decide how best to actually measure the capacity in question, as well as *who* is going to be measured.

A more technical way to describe this process is that the researcher must determine a methodological design for their research, the process they will undertake in order to examine their hypothesis; they must operationalize the construct being examined, that is, define what the construct is and how it will be measured, and then assemble a sample of research subjects who will be measured on the construct, most typically by completing a questionnaire or some such instrument, by being observed performing a task (such as memorizing a list of words, for example), or by being interviewed about their experience.

But as described thus far, this methodological design wouldn't be sufficient for examining a hypothesized relationship between aging and memory, because in its current form only part of the hypothesized relationship has been defined: memory. But what about aging, which is really the point of the research, the hypothesis that with increasing age a change happens in the way we remember certain things? In order to begin to get at whether there is, indeed, a relationship between aging processes and changes in memory capacity (and again, remember it is important to specify what kind of memory capacity), we have to somehow operationally define what we mean by aging in the context of this research. Recall an earlier discussion regarding the limitations of age as a variable and how chronological age serves as a proxy or stand-in for underlying aging

> processes – processes thought to be caused by aging itself, as well as processes associated with increasing age.
>
> How, then, do we go about examining our hypothesis, that aging causes changes in certain memory capacities?

What follows are chapters exploring current perspectives and knowledge organized around the following themes: the aging body; the aging mind; age in society; the political economy of aging; and the meaning of old age. As you read on, we encourage you to apply the foundational ideas and basic concepts we've been discussing thus far. As well, we invite you to ponder the relevance of all of this for your own lived experience as you travel through your life-course and accompany others as they travel through theirs.

BIBLIOGRAPHY

Achenbaum, W.A. (1995). *Crossing frontiers: Gerontology emerges as a science.* Cambridge University Press: New York, NY.

Bengtson, V.L., & Schaie, K.W. (Eds.) (1999). *Handbook of theories of aging.* Springer Publishing Company: New York, NY.

Blackburn, J.A., & Dulmus, C.N. (2007). *Handbook of gerontology: Evidence-based approaches to theory, practice, and policy.* John Wiley & Sons: Hoboken, NJ.

Bloom, D.E., Canning, D., & Lubet, A. (Spring 2015). Global Population Aging: Facts, Challenges, Solutions & Perspectives. *Daedalus, 144(2),* 80–92.

Dannefer, D., & Phillipson, C. (2010). *The Sage handbook of social gerontology.* Sage: Los Angeles, CA.

de Medeiros, K. (2014). Who "Owns" Gerontology? The Importance of Thinking Beyond the Sciences. *The Gerontologist, 54(4),* 723–727.

Estes, C.L., Binney, E.A., & Culbertson, R.A. (1992). The Gerontological Imagination: Social Influences on the Development of Gerontology, 1945–Present. *International Journal of Aging and Human Development, 35(1),* 49–65.

Ferraro, K.F. (2006). Imaging the Disciplinary Advancement of Gerontology: Whither the Tipping Point? *The Gerontologist, 46(5),* 571–573.

Ferraro, K.F. (2007). Is Gerontology Interdisciplinary? *Journal of Gerontology: Social Sciences, 62B(1),* S2.

Ferraro, K., & Wilmoth, J. (Eds.) (2013). *Gerontology: Perspectives and issues* (4th edition). Springer Publishing Company: Secaucus, NJ.

Gullette, M.M. (2004). *Aged by culture*. The University of Chicago Press: Chicago, IL.

Hendricks, J., & Achenbaum, A. (1999). "Historical Development of Theories of Aging," in V.L. Bengtson & K. Warner Schaie (eds.), *Handbook of theories of aging*. pp. 21–39. Springer Publishing Company: New York, NY.

Johnson, M.L. (Ed.) (2005). *The Cambridge handbook of age and ageing*. Cambridge University Press: Cambridge, UK.

Katz, S. (1996). *Disciplining old age: The formation of Gerontological knowledge*. University Press Virginia: Charlottesville, VA.

Kivnick, H.Q., & Pruchno, R. (2011). Bridges and boundaries: Humanities and arts enhance gerontology. *The Gerontologist, 51(2)*, 142–144.

National Institute on Aging. (2007). *Why population aging matters: A global perspective*. National Institutes on Health: USA, Publication No. 07-6134, March.

Olshansky, S.J., & Carnes, B.A. (2001). *The quest for immortality: Science at the frontiers of aging*. W.W. Norton & Company: New York, NY.

Olshansky, S.J. (Spring 2015). The Demographic Transformation of America. *Daedalus, 144(2)*, 13–19.

2

THE AGING BODY

When Prince Gautama Buddha first left the protected palace where he grew up, he saw three disturbing sights by the side of the road: a sick man, an old person, and a dead body. By discovering sickness, old age, and death, the Buddha was shocked into the search that eventually led him to enlightenment. As it turns out, these three phenomena – aging, sickness, and death – are all connected. Aging increases the probability of sickness – Alzheimer's, cancer, cardio-vascular disease and all the rest. Whether by sickness or by acci-dent, aging ends with death. It was this fact that the Buddha understood. It is something we all understand, even if dimly and even if reluctantly. But more to the point – and this is perhaps the deeper lesson from the Buddha's awakening – it isn't the incontro-vertible fact that each of us will experience sickness, aging, and eventually death that is the problem, but the suffering we experi-ence in contemplating and accepting our own frailty and imperma-nence. But we shall postpone discussing the *meaning* of adult aging and old age, and our feelings about our travels into later life, until a later chapter. For now, let's turn to how Gerontology attends to the aging body.

We recognize what sickness is whenever we get sick and then get well. We know that from childhood. We recognize death, too, especially as we get older. But what is aging? The question itself reminds us of St. Augustine, who once was asked, What is time? He replied, when no one asks me, I know what it is. When I am asked, I do not know what it is. So it is with aging: we think we know, but defining it proves harder than we might imagine.

Aging is not simply the passage of time. When we ask about how organisms grow old, we are not asking a question about the passage of time. Time passes for rocks and mountains; they may erode but we do not speak of them as "growing old." For trees and dogs and humans – for all living things – we can speak about aging. Aging unfolds over time, and many of us mark our travels through the life-course by anchoring our experiences to certain periods of time, but aging is not caused by the passage of time itself. Nor is aging the same thing as dying. Aging is part of living, though the terminus of the aging process is, ultimately, death.

Clearly, questions about the biology of aging must be framed carefully! It is not the mere passage of time but other changes that we ascribe to the aging of living organisms, for example, vulnerability to sickness or death. A clear example of this is **Gompertz Law** (see Figure 2.1). In the 19th century, Gompertz discovered that the human death rate doubles about every eight years. The rule of mortality rates doubling over time suggests that something more than mere accident is involved here: but what is it?

Scientists have long sought for some objective "clock" in an organism that could give a definitive measure of intrinsic aging, something endogenous happening beyond the passage of time alone. **Bio-markers** are specific biological indicators that change with age and could therefore become a standard measure for the rate of aging. But such bio-markers are not easily found.

We can think about the biology of aging in different ways at different scales: from the molecular up through cells, tissues and whole organisms. If we go below the level of molecules to atoms, then at all scales of human time, atoms remain virtually changeless. We can even speak of aging at the level of whole populations – as we did in a previous chapter in speaking of "population aging" and increases in the average life expectancy during the past century. But that term, in another way, is a metaphor: populations don't "age" in the same way as cells, organs or whole organisms. Still, population aging is an

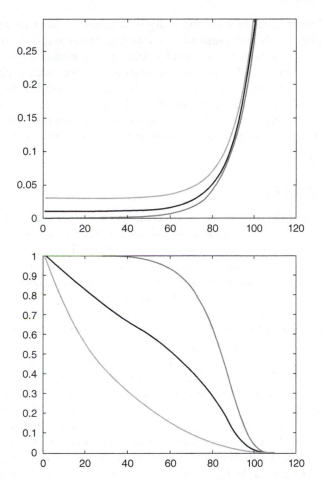

Figure ·2.1 Example of a Gompertz curve depicting chance of death with increasing age

important consideration when looking at the social aspects of aging, to which we will return in a later chapter.

For now, we will follow an approach inspired by the classic film "Powers of Ten," where we consider how biological aging appears at different levels of scale and analysis: moving up from molecules to higher levels and eventually whole organisms and species. We can recognize how the molecules that are the building blocks of life – proteins and DNA – are vulnerable and not easily replaced. Molecules are repaired and cells do die and are replaced. But not indefinitely so. As we move up the scale of size, we can recognize how increased vulnerability – to sickness and eventually death – may give us a key to finally understanding, at the biological level, what aging is.

MOLECULES

We start at the smallest scale: molecules. Can we say that molecules are subject to aging? What about atoms, the building blocks of molecules? Some atoms – for example, radioactive elements – are subject to decay over time. But we would not describe radioactive decay as aging. Some molecules could be described as vulnerable and subject to instability, because of weak chemical bonds. An example of an unstable molecule is nitroglycerine. There are molecular ions, too, that are not stable. But here again that vulnerability would not typically be described as "aging."

The question about aging molecules becomes evident when we consider the distinctive building blocks of all living organisms. Living organisms are material organizations of organic molecules. The most important of these are proteins, the building blocks of life, and the genetic molecules that comprise the blueprint of living things (DNA and RNA). Some protein molecules last only minutes, while others last a few weeks. Proteins like albumin need to be replaced regularly. A few proteins in the body, such as those in the enamel of teeth, can last an entire lifetime.

The DNA molecule is the key to reproduction and, as known since Watson and Crick, cell division works by means of DNA dividing and replicating itself. But the process of replication by DNA is not perfect. Mistakes happen, just as we might see in a photocopy reproduction done repeatedly. In the case of DNA, our bodies have vigorous molecular repair mechanisms to fix damage to DNA. But not all errors are repaired, and we see an accumulation of these errors with aging.

Repairing the errors in DNA replication is not cost free. Living organisms can be described as complex islands of order ("negative entropy"), maintained by free energy ultimately provided by the sun. The process of metabolism, for both plants and animals, involves a complex energy cycle based on oxygen and sugar. Could the price of using oxygen in metabolism be the key to aging?

Some molecular variants of oxygen, those known as radicals, have an electrical charge that makes them damaging to other key organic molecules, including proteins and DNA. Thus, the intrinsic process of energy production in living organisms can itself be the origin of some of the damage inflicted on the essential molecular structures that keep us alive. Biological aging, then, is not an "accident" but something akin to the "cost of doing business" by living organisms. Aging is not the mere passage of time but the cumulative damage, and vulnerability, arising from the biological processes that keep us alive.

Free radicals are atoms with unpaired electrons and they are very reactive. Free radicals are formed in many chemical reactions, including those in normal metabolism. Those ionized oxygen molecules cause damage because they more readily bond with proteins and other physiological structures. Sometimes the proteins become inactive and unable to carry out their functions. As these move around the cell, free radicals can destroy disulfide bonds and promote destructive protein cross-linking. They can also encourage abnormal lipids to form. Free radicals can also react with DNA, damaging this critical genetic code structure. The results of these developments will be to damage enzyme production and weaken energy production or to damage cell membranes, which is an aging-related change.

A similar mechanism of physical aging is **glycosylation**. Among the most universal of all chemical changes in living things are those involving sugar (glucose). Like oxygen, glucose is fundamental for metabolism. But, like oxygen, it has a down side. When foods such as meat and bread are heated, the proteins combine with sugar and turn brown, in a process known as caramelization. In our bodies, the sticky by-products of this same chemical reaction can literally gum up our cells. Glycosylation could prove to be the basis for damage appearing as adult-onset diabetes, as well as stiffened joints and blocked arteries.

For many years, it has been believed that free radicals are an important cause of aging because free radicals generated by ordinary metabolism can damage cell structures. If so, it was thought, then antioxidants in our diet could help protect us against damage associated with aging. It is true that antioxidants can be beneficial in helping foodstuffs maintain taste and color and remain edible longer. The critical issue is lipid peroxidation, referring to oxidative degradation of fats (lipids) arising from the impact of free radicals on lipids in cell membranes. But, based on evidence to date, it remains uncertain whether antioxidants actually slow the process of aging. In some cases, high levels of the antioxidant Vitamin E can actually cause cancer.

Observers going back to Aristotle have noted that different plants and animals have very different lifespans. The fly does not live as long as a dog, and the dog does not live as long as the tortoise. Aristotle noted that very large animals – such as an elephant – tend to be more long-lived than very small ones, like rodents. Differences across species suggest that aging and longevity are under the control of our genes. Some of the strongest evidence for the genetic control of aging comes from research on the *c. elegans* roundworm. Biologists discovered that by altering a few important genes, they have been able to increase the lifespan of the worm by up to ten times, while also limiting many of the deficits of aging. Genetic damage is most probably a central cause of biological aging.

One in four of you reading this book has a specific genetic time bomb that makes you three to ten times more susceptible to developing late-onset Alzheimer's. The gene is known as the apolipoprotein E4 (ApoE4). If you inherit a single variant of ApoE4 from one parent, your Alzheimer's risk triples. If you inherit a double dose from both parents, your risk rises by ten times. Since we don't know the cause of Alzheimer's Disease, and there is no cure, it's understandable that many people don't want to know if they are carrying the ApoE4 gene. But the genetic link raises important questions and has implications for biological research on genetics and aging.

Clearly genes, perhaps "longevity genes," play a big role in shaping aging and longevity, and scientists are only just beginning to understand their impact. But to make matters more complex we may need to look beyond the structure of genes and DNA or the interaction between the nucleus and the proteins in a cell. Aging may require us to look at **epigenetics**, that is, the variations in cellular behavior and physiological traits that come about because of environmental forces that switch on (or off) the genes in our cells. In other words, we need to go beyond one-way reductionism (small to large) and think instead of interactions between levels. Genes retain transcriptional potential, but it may be much harder to find pathways to aging at the level of cells, tissues, organs and whole organisms. It is to these levels that we now turn.

CELLS

When we come to the level of cells we can certainly speak of "cellular aging." Cells typically divide (mitosis), but not forever. Normal cells, in a laboratory setting, will die after approximately 50 divisions. This limited number of divisions is known as the **Hayflick Limit**, in honor of the biologist who discovered it in 1961, Leonard Hayflick. But some cells are potentially immortal and could keep dividing forever, such as germ cells (reproductive cells) and also, ominously, cancer cells.

Cells do not all age in the same way. For example, red blood cells do not have a nucleus and are replaced every four months. By contrast, neurons and skeletal cells are present in the body throughout life. As terminally differentiated cells, they characteristically do not die. Cells are turning over all the time, and they are also aging. There are many different mechanisms of aging taking place in cells.

Within the cell there are specific smaller structures implicated in aging. For example, mitochondria are the power source within cells. Mitochondria change their shape with aging, which may imply diminished energy with aging. **Lipofuscin** is a kind of "debris" that accumulates in cells with aging and it may interfere with cell function over the course of aging. But lipofuscin doesn't accumulate in all cells of the body. The accumulation of lipofuscin is a distinctive hallmark of aging and accumulation of this "debris" occurs at a rate inversely related to longevity. It turns out that accumulation of lipofuscin is linked to macular degeneration, a degenerative disease of the eye that is age-related, though not caused by normal aging itself.

How long can cells live? Can we speak of aging at the cellular level? When cells from an older animal are transplanted into a petri dish, they divide fewer times. It was once believed that cells could replicate or replace themselves indefinitely. But Hayflick discovered that, in tissue culture in a petri dish, a normal human cell would only divide between 40 and 60 times, and no more. After that point, the cell becomes senescent or aging.

Is there a distinctive "clock" to measure the rate of cellular senescence? It appears that there is. In both humans and other animals, cellular senescence can be recognized by tiny structures in the cell known as **telomeres** (see Figure 2.2). Telomeres are the "caps" on the tips of chromosomes. In each cycle of cell division, telomeres get shorter. Reduction in the length of telomeres has been shown to be linked to biological aging. A specific enzyme in the nucleus of the cell, telomerase, works constantly to rebuild the tips of chromosomes. Telomeres have a paradoxical relationship with cancer. Telomere shortening may prevent cancer in human cells by limiting the number of cell divisions. At the same time, shortened telomeres could impair immune function and increase vulnerability to cancer. For this reason, it seems unlikely that simply introducing telomerase or interfering with telomeres alone will in itself slow the process of aging.

But why do telomeres shrink over time? Nobel Prize winner Elizabeth Blackburn estimates that the majority of reduction is caused by genetic factors, while the rest is influenced by environmental factors such as diet, stress or environmental threats. In families with a genetic predisposition toward lower telomerase production, family members typically suffer from age-related diseases and they die earlier. But chronic stress can also be a factor. People under great stress – such as mothers of children with disabilities or those subject to trauma – also have shortened telomeres. In short, aging at the level of telomeres is determined by a combination of genetic and environmental factors. Shortened telomeres seem to prevent further cell multiplication, in keeping with the Hayflick Limit.

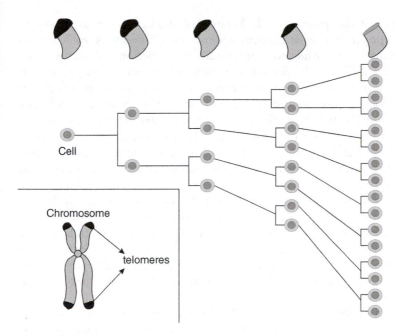

Figure 2.2 Telomeres as we age

We have seen that DNA can be damaged and that repair is neither cost free nor completely successful. We do not know exactly how DNA damage and repair contribute to aging. But we do know that the risk of cancer goes up exponentially with advancing age. It is important to note that damage to DNA happens in the telomeres and the damage is not fully repaired. We can see the impact of damaged or shrinking telomeres at the level of the organism. For example, mice whose telomeres have become shortened will have lower lifespans.

The process of aging can be seen at the level of cells which, after the Hayflick Limit, go into senescence. Aging occurs at the molecular level, and damage to molecules, such as DNA, will eventually result in aging to structures at the cellular level. A good example of this is the process of deliberate cell death, known as apoptosis. **Apoptosis** is what happens when a cell self-destructs, or "commits suicide" according to a programmed instruction. We can surmise that if these cells did not die, they might cause damage, such as impairing the function of mitochondria, the powerhouse of cells, or produce protein misfolding. This loss of an individual cell may come about because the cell has accumulated internal damage, for example, has become malignant. By destroying itself – the act of "cell suicide" – the cell prevents loss at the higher level of organs. Interestingly, biologists have discovered that rates of cell death can increase with age.

Our bodies constantly replace old cells with new ones at the rate of millions per second. By the time you finish reading this sentence, 50 million of your cells will have died and been replaced by others. Some are lost through "wear and tear"; some just reach the end of their life; and others deliberately self-destruct. The life cycle of every cell is carefully controlled, so you should always have just the right number of each type of cell.

But different kinds of cells differ in their life expectancy. For example, red blood cells will live for only about four months, while white blood cells survive for more than a year. Skin cells remain alive for two to three weeks. Crucial here is the survival of cells in the nervous system: brain cells typically last an entire lifetime and neurons in the cerebral cortex are not replaced when they die.

TISSUES AND SYSTEMS

It isn't necessary to read a book on Gerontology to be aware that people tend to become more frail as they get older. **Frailty** can be interpreted in various ways, but the most obvious meaning is vulnerability to assaults or damage of any kind to the body. Another way to describe this trend is to speak of declining **reserve capacity** of biological systems. Technically, we can describe this as declining reserve capacity – the ability to "bounce back" or be resilient – and this in itself could be taken as a key definition of biological aging.

Of great importance is the human immune system, which tends to become less robust with aging. For example, aging tends to weaken the power of T-lymphocytes. This pattern is seen in organs such as the thymus, lymph nodes, spleen and bone marrow. The role of the immune system is central to understanding the vulnerabilities of old age. For example, the same illness − such as pneumonia − could strike a 10-year-old or an 80-year-old. But the 80-year-old is far more likely to die from the disease, both because of weakness of the lungs and because the overall immune system is not as strong as it was earlier in life.

A related phenomenon is the role of inflammation in tissues. Chronic, low-grade inflammation is known to be closely linked to the diseases associated with aging and perhaps even with biological aging itself, but it is not clear what is the cause or effect here. To speak of "immunosenescence" is to emphasize that the inflammatory response of the body is tightly controlled by our immune system in all its complexity. There are multiple control systems involved here, and the study of inflammation has become central to current research in the biology of aging.

Muscles, bones and joints are all susceptible to deterioration in later life. For example, the muscle system with advancing age becomes susceptible to **sarcopenia**, or degeneration of muscle mass and loss of both strength and quality. From the time we are born up until age 30, our muscles grow stronger. But with each decade after that we are liable to lose up to 4 percent of muscle mass, and this loss can accelerate after age 75. The result can be frailty and likelihood of falling. But, here again, we should not think of sarcopenia as inevitable: it is certainly influenced by diet and exercise, for example. Strength resistance training has been shown to be helpful in reducing sarcopenia into advanced old age.

A similar process happens with bones. Humans typically lose bone mass and density with advancing age. The result can be **osteoporosis**. For women, the hormonal changes that come with menopause can be a specific marker for increased bone loss, resulting in vulnerability to fractures. While menopause is a normal part of female aging, osteoporosis is not. However, hip fractures are a common cause of need for long-term care.

The aging of bone and muscle is often invisible to us. But the aging of the skin is much more apparent. We all know that adult aging tends to bring wrinkles. With advancing age, the skin becomes

Image 2.1 Facing Aging

Credit: By 芝崖 (http://cc.nphoto.net/view/2008/12597.shtml) [CC BY 2.5 cn (http://creativecommons.org/licenses/by/2.5/cn/deed.en)], via Wikimedia Commons.

thinner and drier. Here, too, we can attribute these visible manifest-ations to aging at the biological level. Connective tissues over time show a decline in elasticity, because of changes in collagen. This trend is reflected in wrinkles, tightened joints and other parts of the body – things we notice on an everyday level when we speak about the aging of the body. Cross-linking of collagen molecules is the ultimate cause of this process. Most of what we see, visibly, as "aging" is the result of cross-linking of proteins (as well as environmental exposure; we must remember that many of the changes that happen to the body as we age are a complex interaction between the "inside" – genetic and biological processes – and "outside" – environmental, social and behavioral factors).

ORGANS

Many organs in the human body show declining function with chronological age. For example, the term **vital capacity** refers to the maximum amount of air that can be breathed in and out by the lungs, and this tends to decline with age. Blood pressure, too, tends to rise with age, and high blood pressure (hypertension) is a significant risk factor for kidney disease, stroke and other serious chronic conditions that are **age-associated**.

Different organs of the body exhibit different distinctive changes with biological aging. The organs of the reproductive system after midlife show dramatic signs of aging: prominently menopause and the end of fertility for females. In males, too, we see changes in hormone levels, though not as apparent as female menopause. With advancing age, the eye is more susceptible to cataracts and macular degeneration. With aging, kidney function tends to decrease as well. In the lungs as well as in the kidneys we can speak of a loss of reserve capacity, or the ability of the organism to meet peak-load demands, as during vigorous physical exercise. Diminished reserve capacity may not have any discernible impact on the normal activities of daily living. For instance, not having reserves to run a marathon race is probably irrelevant to most activities of daily life (unless, that is, you are a Master marathon runner!).

Brain aging is of vital importance for animals because the brain is the fundamental control center for the nervous system. The brain is sensitive to changes in energy metabolism because, even at rest, the brain consumes up to one-fifth of all energy production in the body. The brain cannot store energy as glycogen or fat the way other parts of the body are able to do. Distinctive age-associated disorders like Parkinson's and Alzheimer's Disease are affected by dietary energy intake, but studies with non–human animals, such as rats, do not necessarily translate into knowledge that can be applied to the human brain.

For human animals, executive function in the brain is of the greatest importance and this function may be at risk with advanced age. For example, working memory, reasoning, problem-solving and other cognitive processes can be damaged, resulting in **dementia**. One of the most profound forms of dementia is Alzheimer's Disease, named by neurologist Dr. Alois Alzheimer in 1906.

The causes of dementia can be multiple, including **cerebral vascular dysfunction** involving small strokes that damage brain tissue over time. Investigators into Alzheimer's have long pursued the **Amyloid Hypothesis**, which has received support from the fact that plaques and tangles in the brain of Alzheimer's patients show a distinctive deposition of the amyloid protein. Yet the now famous Nun Study, captured by David Snowdown in his book *Aging with grace* (2002), looked at autopsy results and failed to find a causal relationship between plaques and tangles and the functional manifestations of Alzheimer's Disease. It seems clear that Alzheimer's and other forms of dementia result from some form of neurodegeneration, though there are individual differences in how these structural changes affect functioning. Yet a definitive cause or cure for the disease has not been found.

When speaking about brain aging, we need to identify losses but also recognize the capacity of the brain for resilience and recovery of function – another unexpected finding from the Nun Study. This process is known as **neuroplasticity**. Until recently, it was mistakenly believed that, after growth in childhood and early life, the brain remains unchanged into adulthood. Since nerve cells do not reproduce, an unchangeable brain would be susceptible to losses. It is now recognized that the brain has a capacity for neuroplasticity, permitting recovery from losses. Neuroscientists recognize that, even into later adulthood, the brain can recover from damage and also change in response to positive environmental stimuli and lifelong learning.

ORGANISM

We have seen that it is possible to identify the biological process of aging at many levels: from the molecular, to the cell, to tissues, organs, and whole systems of the body. What about the organism as a whole? We certainly see biological aging at the total organism level. We can even speak of **normal aging**, meaning simply something akin to the Gompertz Law: death rates increase with age and so do rates of illness and frailty. But aside from mortality, the human body shows distinctive age-related changes such as:

- declining fertility among women over age 35;
- diminished eyesight, perhaps caused by loss of elasticity in the lens;
- some degree of arthritis, in a majority of those in their sixties; and
- rising risk of neurogenerative diseases such as dementia.

Thus, we come to a basic biological question: why is this so? Why do organisms exhibit decline in functional capacity in different systems over time? That decline doesn't happen, say, with drinking glasses or other material objects. These objects remain vulnerable in the same way at every point in time. But living systems, certainly human beings, increase their vulnerability with time.

One explanation for this process is what is known as the principle of **antagonistic pleiotropy**. This idea is that certain genetically determined traits could be beneficial for survival early in life but become harmful at later ages. For example, people likely to have sickle-cell anemia are less likely to contract malaria: thus, they survive one ailment but become vulnerable to another. Similarly, there can be a genetic protection against some vulnerability in youth but that causes greater vulnerability in old age. According to the idea of natural selection, survival will be favored to the age of reproduction. It is possible that many of the disorders seen in old age can be explained by this principle of genetic determination of traits in youth or in old age.

Caloric restriction is the reduction in the amount of daily calorie intake, a process that has evidently slowed the rate of aging in invertebrates, birds and mammals. Experiments on roundworms, mice and rats showed that feeding animals fewer calories resulted in longer lifespans. However, the results do not appear to apply to primates, as shown by a 25-year study conducted by the National Institute on Aging in the US. Biologists now tend to believe that caloric restriction is unlikely to enhance longevity in humans.

There are gender differences in life expectancy. More males than females are conceived, but the death rate for human males is higher than females at every age, even before birth. But this genetic difference is far overshadowed by environmental factors over the life-course. Historically, female mortality was higher than males because of risk associated with childbirth. And still today, gender discrimination of various kinds in many countries will contribute to deaths for women. But overall, in economically developed countries, life expectancy at birth is around 79 years for males and 83 years for females (slightly less in the US, slightly more in Japan).

SPECIES

We know that there are dramatic differences in the longevity of different species. There are no 100-year-old dogs or 40-year-old mice. On the other hand, there are 100-year-old tortoises, which can even live to be 150 years or more. The famous California Redwood tree can live to be 2,000 years old, while the mayfly typically dies on the same day it becomes an adult. Evidently, there is a genetic control on the maximum lifespan of different species.

Maximum lifespan seems to increase in relation to brain size. But lifespan is also related to the length of period of growth to sexual maturity. Body size is also a factor, for example, bigger animals, like elephants, tend to live longer. Brain weight in relation to total body weight seems to be a key: the bigger the brain, the longer the animal will live. But biologists have long puzzled about why these mathematical ratios exist and what they signify.

Biologists suggest that DNA repair rates are linked to maximum longevity, perhaps through basal metabolic rate (BMR). BMR is an estimate of calories at rest used over a period of time. In essence, BMR designates the least amount of energy needed to keep someone alive. BMR varies across species. For example, a mouse or a hummingbird has a very high metabolic rate. A mouse's heart beats 600 times a minute – 10 times the rate of a human being. A hummingbird can have a heartbeat rate of up to 1,200 beats per minute. Slower metabolism is linked to longevity.

Consider the case of the hydra, a simple, freshwater animal akin to jellyfish. Do hydras age at all or are they, in principle, immortal? Flatworms, or Platyhelminthes, could also be described as "almost immortal" because of their great regeneration capacity. Lobsters are sometimes called immortal because they don't slow down or weaken (though they do get eaten!). The death rate for hydra does not increase as a function of time. Like all organisms, hydra cells are continually dividing and replicating themselves by cell division (mitosis). Perhaps significantly, telomeres in their cells retain the same length with age, unlike the case of human telomeres.

There clearly is a genetic basis for how long multicellular organisms can live. More than thirty years ago, biologists identified a single gene, which they named age-1, in the nematode worm. By inducing a deliberate change or mutation in that gene, they were able to induce a 40 percent increase in the lifespan of the worm. Other genes related to longevity, in organisms ranging from fruit flies to mice, have also been identified. For long-lived humans, the FOXO3 gene has been receiving a great deal of scrutiny. But even these big gains in longevity do not mean that aging has been defeated.

As we've discussed, a key element in biological aging is the accumulation of damage to proteins, genes, and other essential structures in our bodies. In human beings, the result of biological aging differs dramatically among individuals. In geriatric medicine, there is a well-known saying that, unlike the predictable profile of a 2-year-old ("the terrible twos"), "If you've seen one 80-year-old, you've seen one 80-year-old."

There has been no change in maximum lifespan since human beings evolved in their modern form, perhaps 100,000 years ago. Accidents, disease or failure to maintain homeostasis – diminished biological reserve capacity – remain the major reasons for death. As we discussed previously, life expectancy has increased dramatically in the past century, and there are more very long-lived people (e.g., centenarians) than ever before. But maximum lifespan hasn't changed.

There are announcements on the Internet claiming that the first person to live to age 150 has already been born. Biogerontologist Aubrey de Grey has gone further, claiming that the first person to live to be 1,000 has probably already been born. De Grey specifically looks forward to "the defeat of aging," and he expects defeat to come before too long.

No one has proven that de Grey is wrong. All we can say for sure is that the maximum that any human being has ever been proven to live was documented in the case of the French woman, Jeanne Calment, who died at the age of 122. Other claims to greater age are possible but have never been proven. In economically developed countries there are fewer than two centenarians for every 10,000 people today. The prospects for becoming a "super-centenarian" (living to 110 or 120) are even smaller. Your odds may be better than winning the lottery, but not by much. In the hope-springs-eternal department, we may include Silicon Valley venture capitalists now bankrolling new anti-aging research. Their interest makes sense since they believe that hundreds of billions of dollars are possible from a breakthrough in so-called anti-aging technology. But it is useful to remember that, to date, none of the anti-aging products on the market thus far have ever worked.

CONCLUSION

It is often said that today we're living longer than ever. The claim is only partly true. Life expectancy has certainly gone up, but not by as much as people believe. In the first place, **life expectancy**, or average time expected to live, is different from maximum age or **lifespan** which is characteristic of each species. Average life expectancy, in economically developed countries, has gone up dramatically in the 20th century – from 48 years to 78 years, on average. But this gain has mostly been the result of preventing infectious disease in childhood or similar interventions. Even if we were to find a cure for cancer tomorrow, it would not increase life expectancy by much at all. We are left with a basic question: Why do our bodies age at all?

Many theories have been advanced for why we age. Some have argued that aging and death are an evolutionary mechanism for removing declining organisms from the gene pool. Others have pointed to the Hayflick Limit, suggesting that aging is built into our cells. It turns out that most animals have around the same number of heartbeats in their lifetime. But very large animals have hearts that beat slower, so perhaps this is why they tend to live longer.

Among mammals, humans are among the most long-lived. But other species can live far longer: a lobster can live up to 170 years, a koi fish for 200 years. Among plants, the Bristlecone pine can live to be 4,600 years: in other words, it may have been just a seedling at the time the pyramids were raised in Egypt. As we have already seen, a hydra or jellyfish are potentially immortal.

August Weismann, the great German biologist of the 19th century, put forward the central question of biological aging: Why aren't all of our (somatic) cells endowed with the same kind of "immortality" enjoyed by germ cells? Here lies the basic challenge to increasing human longevity. Cumulative damage to cells and organs takes place over time, and age-related diseases like cancer or Alzheimer's increase with age. In fact, the two are related because it is cumulative damage that creates vulnerability to illnesses. Over time, mutations in cells will lead to illnesses that prove fatal, as happens with cancer. Cancer cells are produced in our body all the time and are eliminated by our immune system, but with advancing age, the protective immune response becomes less resilient. Thomas Kirkwood, author of the "disposable soma" idea of aging, posits that there is a trade-off in the way the organism protects germ cells (sperm and egg) versus the ordinary (somatic) cells of the body.

There has always been debate about whether it is nature or nurture, genes or environment, which cause the body to age. Again, the answer is "both." In this chapter, we have moved from the very small scale – macromolecules such as DNA and proteins – up through organelles and the nucleus within cells, up through tissues, organs and systems that are part of the whole organism. It is tempting to imagine that causes at the small scale are fully responsible for events, like aging, that are visible at the level of the whole organism. But we have seen that stress experienced at the large scale can actually affect the size of telomeres at the sub-cellular level. In other words, causality does not operate just from small to large, but in both directions and in complex ways that we've only just begun to understand.

For more than three decades, both scientists and the public have been fascinated by the idea of **compression of morbidity**, proposed by Dr James F. Fries, a Stanford University physician. The idea of compression of morbidity is that people could remain healthy up until the last month or year of life, then die rapidly of natural causes. The record since then has been ambiguous: some people do live – and die – according to a compression of morbidity model, but others experience a prolongation of morbidity, for example, being saved from a heart attack at age 75 only to linger for years with dementia or other conditions.

Gerontologists who study the biology of aging have been attracted by the idea of slowing the biological processes of aging, both to raise the average life expectancy toward the maximum lifespan possible and also to enable people to live a healthy life during those extended years: more years *and* better years. As we have seen in looking at the lifespans of other organisms, there is wide variation in longevity. What if it were possible to extend "**health span**" and not just increase life expectancy? What if it were possible for people to live even beyond the 122-year-old limit *and* to live in good health?

Biologists attracted to the idea of slowing the processes of aging believe that conventional medicine is taking a limited, fragmentary approach, attacking one disease after another: first cancer, then Alzheimer's and so on for other chronic diseases associated with aging and old age. Some Biogerontologists believe that it would be more fruitful to look at fundamental biological factors that are the foundation of biological aging itself, such as low-grade inflammation, unrepaired damage to DNA, and the degradation of cells documented by the Hayflick Limit.

We have explored in this chapter how there are different mechanisms of aging going on at different levels of the body. When we look at the process of aging from the small scale – molecules, genes and cells – up to the large scale – tissues, organs, and whole organisms – we come back, again and again, to the question of cause and consequence. For example, biologists know that with the processes of aging there is a decline in biochemical pathways that protect cells from misfolded proteins. Misfolded proteins do coincide with aging. But which is cause and which is effect? There is debate on that question. We know that the length of telomeres is linked to aging. But telomeres can become shorter because of stress or poor nutrition. So again, we must ask: which is the cause and which is the effect? So too, with genetics and epigenetics: there are more connections between large and small than might have been imagined. As we look at aging at multiple levels, we see a bewildering complex of changes: there are dysfunction of proteins, damage to DNA, and changes both within cells and across tissues in the body. At each level, there are multiple pathways and there are causal connections between levels.

In this chapter, following the plan inspired by the classic film "Powers of Ten," we have looked at how biological aging appears at different levels of scale: moving up from molecules to higher levels and eventually whole organisms and species. Those molecules that are the building blocks of life – proteins and DNA – are themselves vulnerable. Molecules are repaired, cells are replaced, and the whole organism has remarkable capacity for protection and renewal. But aging and finitude are deeply embedded in organic structures at all levels of life.

As the Buddha did when he left the protected palace where he grew up, we discover in biological aging a process that raises some of the biggest questions biology can confront: How do the different levels of life interact with each other? Are there hidden "costs" for living on glucose and oxygen? Are there potencies in the "immortal" jellyfish or the ancient Bristlecone pine that we have not yet discovered? Despite the momentous discoveries of recent decades – such as the structure of the human genome or the role of telomeres – our discoveries inspire new questions, which is always the nature of science. As we saw in the life of the Buddha, discovery of human aging, frailty and finitude is only the beginning of the search.

RECOMMENDED BOOKS

Austad, S.N. (1999). *Why we age: What science is discovering about the body's journey through life.* Wiley: New York.

Kirkwood, T. (2001). *Time of our lives: The science of human aging.* Oxford Unviersity Press: Oxford.

McDonald, R.B. (2013). *Biology of aging.* Garland Science: New York.

Scientific American Editors. (2013). *Forever young: The science of aging.* Scientific American: New York.

Silvertown, J. (2013). *The long and the short of it: The science of life span and aging.* University of Chicago Press: Chicago.

Snowdon, D. (2002). *Aging with grace: What the nun study teaches us about leading longer, healthier, and more meaningful lives.* Bantam books: New York.

BIBLIOGRAPHY

Arking, R. (2007). *Biology of aging: Observations and principles* (3rd edition). Oxford University Press: New York.

Austad, S. (1999). *Why we age: What science is discovering about the body's journey through life.* Wiley: New York.

Finch, C. (2007). *The biology of human longevity.* Academic Press: San Diego.

Hall, S. (2005). *Merchants of immortality: Chasing the dream of human life extension.* Mariner Books: Boston.

Hayflick, L. (1994). *How and why we age.* Ballantine Books: New York.

Kaeberlein, M., & Martin, G. (2015). *Handbook of the biology of aging* (8th edition). Academic Press: San Diego.

McDonald, R.B. (2013). *Biology of aging*. Garland Science: New York.

Morrison, P., & Morrison, P. (1994). *Powers of ten: A book about the relative size of things in the universe and the effect of adding another zero*. Scientific American Library: New York.

Olshansky, S.J., Kirkland, J., & Martin, G. (Eds.) (2015). *Aging: The longevity dividend*. Cold Spring Harbor Laboratory Press: New York.

3

THE AGING MIND

There are many negative stereotypes about aging and older persons. Some ageist stereotypes have a ring of truth to them, but many are false and all stereotypes, even those that are positive, are reductive and damaging. For example, it is true our senses (sight, hearing, taste, touch, smell) tend to weaken in later life. It is also true that the likelihood of illness and death grows higher with advancing age. And short-term memory and other cognitive skills may lose some efficiency. But there are other aspects of who we are and how we move through the world that show continuity: our temperament, basic habits, skills and aptitudes, as well as how we adapt and cope with change and challenges. Personality will tend to be more stable with age. Yet a positive experience of aging depends on resilience and adaptation, capacities that may require us to step out of our habitual ways of doing things. There are qualities such as wisdom and maturity, which may be distinctive strengths of long lives, and we need to appreciate these elements of positive aging as well. Understanding the balance of losses, continuities, and gains in the aging mind is the purpose of this chapter.

LOSSES

As people grow older, they often get worried that, when it comes to cognitive capacity, they are "losing it." Their worry may be a matter of memory, problem-solving, or ability to respond to new technologies, such as digital devices. So, we ask: Does intelligence decline with age? (See Figure 3.1.) The answer is, it depends. There are two basic forms of intelligence to be considered: **fluid intelligence** and **crystallized intelligence**. Fluid intelligence means the ability to solve new problems without reliance on previous knowledge or experience. Crystallized intelligence, by contrast, refers to the cumulative body of experience and skills learned over the course of life. Fluid intelligence, most Psychologists believe, does show some decline after midlife. But crystallized intelligence can actually increase with age.

Questions about losses and gains in intelligence need to be put in the context of adaptation and pragmatic use. As we have seen with the aging body, there are declines in different organ systems. But those declines, including diminished reserve capacity, may not matter for most pragmatic issues of everyday life. The same point holds true for losses of cognitive function. These losses should be put in perspective by recognizing the resilience and reserve capacity of the brain, even in advanced age. Advances in

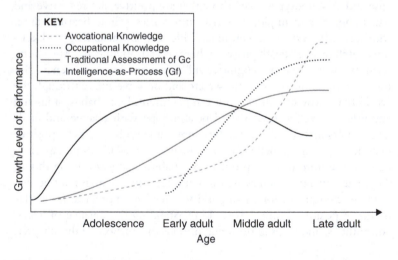

Figure 3.1 Changes in intelligence with age

neuroscience have made clear that neuroplasticity remains a property of the human brain throughout the life-course. At the same time, we know that **plasticity** decreases from childhood through old age while flexibility increases from childhood into middle adulthood (declining somewhat afterward). In old age, neuroplasticity is linked with maintenance, rather than growth. But the main thrust of our understanding today is that the human potential for learning is a lifelong capacity, even into the farthest reaches of old age.

There are recognized declines in cognitive ability with advancing age, although these declines show heterogeneity across individuals. Working memory, which is related to short-term memory, shows a decline with age, and this decline may lead to deficits in so-called **executive function**, that is, one's overall ability to exert control over thinking, attention span, and behavior. These aging-related cognitive declines are closely related to changes in brain structures such as located in the prefrontal cortex or the hippocampus. By contrast, other forms of memory – such as episodic memory or semantic memory – may show very little decline at all with age. The overall pattern here is one that Psychologists have repeatedly identified, for example through intelligence tests given to people of different ages. The result is the so-called **classic aging pattern** where some elements of intellectual functioning decline or slow down with increasing age while others do not.

Much more serious than problems of memory is the condition of **dementia**, which is not the name of a specific disease but rather a name for a group of cognitive deficits including memory failure and loss of problem-solving ability that can impair activities of daily living. The word "senility" is to be avoided, and we should also not think of dementia as part of normal aging. On the contrary, dementia is a brain disorder, the most common form is Alzheimer's Disease. Up to two-thirds of dementia is caused by Alzheimer's, but other causes can be vascular conditions, such as multi-infarct dementia which could be described as a series of very small strokes that eventually damage the brain. Alzheimer's Disease is not easily diagnosed, but it tends to follow a trajectory of stages, beginning with word-finding difficulties or getting lost, and continuing on to the inability to recognize family members. Some forms of Alzheimer's have a familial or genetic component, but medical science does not agree on any clear-cut cause of the disorder.

As we can see from the following diagram (Image 3.1), some effects of Alzheimer's Disease can be documented by neuroimaging techniques, such as with a PET Scan, even though neuroimaging alone does not provide a definitive means of diagnosis:

Contrary to the popular stereotype, we don't "lose a million neurons every day" as we grow older. Most people over age 65 do not suffer from dementia. Rates of cognitive deficit do rise with age, sometimes to the point of mild cognitive impairment (MCI). MCI may be a precursor to full-blown dementia or Alzheimer's Disease, though the research on the connection is still in its early stages. But the progression is by no means inevitable. While the incidence rates for dementias of all kinds increase with advancing age, the overwhelming majority of older people have no mental impairment. Memory defects are quite limited among the vast majority of older people. Nevertheless, some thinking processes do decline or change with age. Cognitive skills such as remembering, solving complex

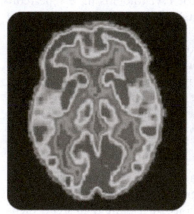 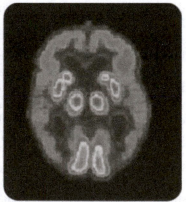

PET Scan of Normal Brain   **PET Scan of Alzheimer's Disease Brain**

Image 3.1 Neuroimaging of Alzheimer's Disease

Credit: By Health and Human Services Department, National Institutes of Health, National Institute on Aging: p. 24[1] (Alzheimer's Disease: Unraveling the Mystery) [Public domain], via Wikimedia Commons.

problems, paying attention, and processing language are affected by age- and disease-related changes in the brain, as mentioned previously.

Cognition has a greater effect than the other types of psychological functioning on the ability to perform the activities of daily living (ADLs). Those who struggle with memory impairments may not be able to keep up with needed medications or remember to turn off the stove when they've finished cooking. They may also find it difficult to make decisions and complete tasks that are often taken for granted, such as paying bills. What's worse, they may lose the ability to recognize their own mental shortcomings. Intervention and compensation is possible here but it may require careful **mental status assessment** by professionals.

Although short-term memory, reaction time, and basic information-processing and problem-solving abilities appear to decline with normal aging, other cognitive functions seem to remain stable or even improve. Wisdom and knowledge about the ways of the world, for example, may become significant strengths as we grow older. In addition, training and practice in problem-solving skills, memory techniques, and other cognitive strategies can noticeably improve the abilities of older people. A good example is driving, where cognitive impairment and slower reaction time can create problems. But, here again, training can strengthen driving skills, enabling very old people to continue driving for more years, even if they adapt, for example, by avoiding driving at night.

The example of changing driving behavior illustrates a more general point: the importance of resilience and adaptation. One form of cognitive adaptation has been called "**selective optimization with compensation**." This phrase means older people who are aging "successfully" may gradually narrow the scope of the capabilities they seek to maintain to those that are most useful, just as we all do throughout our lives. Older people remain adaptive and learn new ways to cope with losses in cognitive functioning. For example, we can keep lists if we are forgetful. And others people may help compensate for losses through a social process dubbed "interactive minds" or "collaborative cognition." We all know that it can be a big mistake to "finish another person's sentence." But stepping in like that could be very helpful to provide support for someone with word-finding problems. The social process of interactive minds is a reason why strong social ties in later life are so important.

Much research remains to be done on cognitive capacity in old age, particularly among the oldest-old. But stereotypes of "senile" or "feebleminded" older adults are not only inadequate, they are damaging. An exaggerated idea of losses makes people who have mild memory failures think that the worst is ahead of them. As one wit put it, "If you forget your keys, that's not a big problem. But if you forget what the keys are for, that's a real problem." People who have an exaggerated fear of the potential losses they may face with aging may actually be setting themselves up for the very challenges that they fear – a self-fulfilling prophesy. There is a substantial body of research suggesting that human beings can suffer psychological decline when they have reduced **locus of control**, that is, the extent to which they feel "in charge" or able to influence things that happen to them. As people age, they are more likely to have chronic health conditions or encounter limits on mobility. The attitude of others – "You're too old for that!" – can reinforce negative expectations. In extreme cases – for example, people living in an institutionalized setting – diminished locus of control can result in excess disability and what has been termed **learned helplessness**. In these situations, it is not surprising that older people will experience significant psychological losses, for example, losing hope or experiencing depression.

This point underscores some of the harmful effects of internalized ageism. The Baltimore Longitudinal Study of Aging is one of the biggest longitudinal studies of aging ever done. Careful analysis of participants looked at adults who were initially healthy and with strong cognitive capacity. But some of those people held negative stereotypes about aging. Those people with negative stereotypes were far more likely to develop features of Alzheimer's Disease later in life, for example, decreased volume in the hippocampus part of the brain and increased plaques and tangles characteristic of Alzheimer's. We know that negative stereotypes about age are common and widely internalized in contemporary culture. Becca Levy's research – Stereotype Embodiment Theory – has shown experimentally that these negative stereotypes can have a profound effect on our behavior and well-being. A more recent study by Robertson and Kenny, which we mentioned in an earlier chapter, supports the idea that negative perceptions of aging can influence physical and cognitive functioning in late life.

Cognitive deficits are not the only losses that can come with age. More than three-quarters of older adults have at least one chronic health condition, and half have two or more. Bereavement and caregiving are predictable challenges of later life as well. Depression is *not* a normal part of aging; it is a mental health issue that can be treated. But risks of depression are more common in later life. Paradoxically, older people may be less likely to be diagnosed or treated for depression. The result can be disastrous. For example, people over the age of 65 are around 14.5 percent of the population of the United States, yet they comprise 18 percent of persons committing suicide. Because of under-reporting, that figure is likely to be even higher. Older men have much higher suicide rates than women, and whites are at greater risk than Blacks. Depression in later life does not have a single cause. But it can often be treated. For example, some depression is caused by polypharmacy – multiple medications taken for conditions like cardiovascular disease or arthritis. Depression can also come as a result of isolation or loss of control. Some of these losses in later life are susceptible to intervention or treatment. We should not assume that late-life depression is a natural part of aging at all.

When considering the losses of aging, it is important to have a realistic, but balanced point-of-view. We should not deny the real challenges and losses that can come with advancing age. But we should also not exaggerate these or imagine that older people lack the ability to compensate for, or adapt to, the challenges that living long can bring. Older people do lose some cognitive capacities, but the losses through normal aging are gradual and for the most part can be accommodated until late in life. What is more, older people often have other cognitive strengths to offer. Their experience of living gives them an understanding of the world and an ability to apply its lessons, which younger people typically have not had time to develop.

CONTINUITIES

In the final scene of Marcel Proust's multi-volume novel, *Remembrance of things past*, all the characters come back together at a costume ball. Proust was repeating an idea put forward by philosopher Arthur Schopenhauer, who said that the closing years of life are like the end of a masquerade party, when the masks are dropped. Anyone who has been to a school reunion can confirm what Proust and Schopenhauer said. At the reunion, we have the shock of seeing people who once young now appear "dressed up" in all the signs of age. Aging researcher Bernice Neugarten believed that as individuals age, they become increasingly like themselves. But we need to ask, What does this continuity mean and where does it come from?

Idea for further exploration:

When does "old age" and "later life" begin?

An interesting informal inquiry you can conduct involves asking persons of different chronological ages and life-course stages at what age they believe "old age" or "later life" begins for *other persons*.

Next, ask at what age they believe "old age" or "later life" begins for *themselves*.

What kinds of answers do you get when persons contemplate the start of their own later life or old age? Are their answers different from when they consider when old age begins for others?

We begin with a basic question: When Does Old Age Start? Psychologist Robert Kastenbaum argued that old age actually begins in infancy, that is, at an early point in life where we respond to events around us in a habitual or mechanical way – what Kastenbaum called "**habituation**." We all know adults who seem "stuck in their ways" and bound by habits more and more with each year of life. Some habits may be helpful. But Kastenbaum was pointing to a tendency to respond to events in an inflexible and predictable way, regardless of what the situation requires. His analysis underscores what it might mean to speak of certain people – even those in middle age – who seem "old before their time." Oldness, in that sense, does not refer to frailty but to an attitude that can keep us from changing and growing as circumstances change. Let us take a moment to point out that the conflation of "oldness" with inflexibility and rigidity is problematic and fundamentally ageist. And yet, the association persists.

As we think about the question "When does old age start?" it may be more useful to consider how people themselves, as they move through the life-course, perceive themselves as having entered into later life and the social status of being an old person. The issue of **age identification** requires attention to self-reports – or what people say about themselves. According to a Pew Research Center's Social and Demographic Trends survey, there is some truth to the idea that "you're only as old as you think you are." For example, in the US, sixty percent of adults aged 65 and over said they feel younger than their actual age, 32 percent said they feel their exact age, and 3 percent said they feel older than their age. Perceptions of the onset of old age vary widely according to the respondent's age. People under 30 believe that old age strikes before the average person turns 60, whereas middle-aged respondents said that old age begins at 70 and adults aged 65 or older put the threshold closer to 74. Perhaps the best conclusion we can draw from these reports is the saying attributed to financier Bernard Baruch: "To me old age is always fifteen years older than I am."

An important element of continuity, over time, in who we are and how we move through the world is personality or basic temperament. According to the "hard plaster" hypothesis, personality traits will tend to stabilize by the age of 30, and this stability has been confirmed by both research and common sense. Investigators have specifically developed a **Five-Factor Model** of personality, described by Costa and McCrae and based on the Baltimore Longitudinal Study of human development. Costa and McCrae have identified neuroticism, extraversion, openness to experience, agreeableness and conscientiousness. These factors have significant implications for aging. For example, extraversion is linked to positive feelings of well-being. Agreeableness tends to increase with age, while neuroticism tends to decrease. Peak conscientiousness in middle age is linked to longevity, which makes sense. People who are conscientious about their health habits are likely to take better care of themselves than people who simply have an optimistic outlook ("It will all work out") toward the future. In sum, continuity in personality traits must be balanced by recognizing that change is always possible, as George Vaillant has documented in the longitudinal research reported in his book *Triumphs of Experience*, based on the Harvard Grant study, to be discussed in more detail below.

Gerontological research suggests that there is no age-related decline in life satisfaction, especially if health is controlled for. Many readers of this book will remember Peter Townshend, singer in the rock group The Who. When he was 20 years old Townshend famously sang the words: "Things they do look awful cold / Hope I die before I get old." Yet Townshend today is now over 70 and has published his "Classical Quadrophenia," a symphonic reimagining of some of his own work from the 1960s. Far from losing creativity with age, he has produced a musical "life-review" and, now that he is old, he has happily been writing his own blog. Despite numerous challenges in life, Peter Townshend seems to be exhibiting qualities of creativity and well-being very different from what he imagined at the age of 20.

Is Townshend an exception? Far from it. Older people generally report higher levels of happiness or life satisfaction than younger people. As people get older, we see a tendency that has been called the **paradox of aging**, namely, people subjectively perceive and report their health status to be stable. They may even report improving health, despite stability in objective health measures. The reasons for this positive subjective attitude are uncertain: perhaps people think of themselves as in better health compared to others of the same age; or perhaps they have an assumption that aging must entail functional decline but they are surprised by how they are functioning or they accept how they are functioning as that which is to be expected. Or, perhaps appreciation for one's life increases as one reaches old age. In any case, there is a clear positivity bias in the subjective experience of aging.

Research seems to suggest that happiness in life is a U-shaped curve: Psychological well-being is highest in early adulthood and late adulthood but at its lowest in midlife, around age 50.

Consistent with the U-shaped curve, the likelihood of depression is greatest between age 40 and 50. Researchers are not sure of the reason, but some argue that, with maturity, people come to acknowledge their genuine strengths and weaknesses. Realistic self-understanding, in turn, is tied to positive emotions. For example, a

General Social Survey from the National Opinion Research Center found that successful aging is linked to positive emotions: saying "yes" to life circumstances. There are older people consumed by regret or disappointment, but emotions like anxiety or anger are actually less likely among older people.

Many of these psychological trends can be seen in the idea of **successful aging**, defined by Rowe and Kahn in three parts: (1) freedom from disease and disability; (2) a high level of both cognitive and physical function; and (3) social and productive engagement. This definition, to some observers, has seemed unduly positive, even unrealistic, since advancing age seems to entail losses. But Rowe and Kahn also offer another definition of successful aging: "**decrement with compensation**," which converges with the idea of resilience and adaptation to deficits. For example, an older person may avoid downhill skiing in favor of cross-country skiing; or a pianist, like the elder Rubenstein, would deliberately play certain passages slower than expected, in order to achieve an effect not otherwise obtained because of physical losses. The point here is that "successful aging" and the related subjective feeling of life satisfaction are *not* correlated with external circumstance or physiological markers of aging. On the contrary, strategies of resilience and adaptation can preserve a positive level of response even into advanced old age.

One way of thinking about the continuity of the aging mind comes from stage theories of human development, including ideas of depth psychology from Sigmund Freud, Carl Jung and Erik Erikson. These approaches from depth psychology consider levels of consciousness and the role of the unconscious in human meaning-making, along with personality structures and defense mechanisms as these evolve over time. The second half of life involves an important dimension of continuity: unresolved conflicts from earlier in life. But in midlife and later life, new challenges present themselves, as well as opportunities to reflect on and resolve past issues and conflicts. In fact, development in later life depends on confronting the past in service to one's present (and future) well-being and integrity. Psychologist Erik Erikson made important contributions to our understanding of the aging mind through his theory of ego psychology and individual identity over the course of life. Erikson's idea of personality is based on a description of distinctive psychological tasks and virtues linked to different stages of life: the so-called "Eight Ages of Man."

These ideas of human development are aligned with the life-course perspective. Erikson built on Freud's psychoanalytic ideas, but developed them in a new direction. For Erikson, infancy and early life were a time to develop qualities of trust in others and, hopefully, to overcome shame and guilt. Adolescence is characteristically a time to forge identity against role confusion. Midlife and later life for Erikson are described as a time for generativity – or, as one Psychologist put it, "outliving the self." Finally, in old age, for Erikson, there is a time where psychological conflict continues, specifically, the struggle between ego-integrity (affirmation of one's life) versus despair. Erikson's idea of ego-integrity is close to what Psychologist Carl Jung described as the primary psychological task of the second half of life, namely, **individuation**, becoming the person you were meant to be and cultivating self-acceptance. The psychology of individuation makes sense because of the well-established fact about growing heterogeneity or individual differences as people move through the life-course.

GAINS

So far in this chapter on the aging mind we have considered the losses that seem to come as we travel through the life-course, as well as ways in which we experience continuity, as we grow older. It is important to keep all these in mind when we consider whether there are also gains that can come in later life. Is it possible that the losses and gains are actually related to each other, as yin and yang in the famous Chinese image? (See Image 3.2.)

The balance between losses and gains brings us to the question of wisdom. Neuropsychologist Elkhonon Goldberg has described this yin–yang relationship as "the wisdom paradox." Goldberg argues, in effect, that the mind can grow stronger as the brain grows older. But this process of developing into deep old age is not automatic, but requires us to make a decision about how we will embrace our aging, to wit, not all elders are wise (and not all younger persons are lacking in wisdom). With advancing age, we can draw on knowledge from prior experience in order to make good decisions.

Image 3.2 Yin and Yang – The Balance Between Losses and Gains
Credit: By Klem [Public domain], via Wikimedia Commons.

We can reflect on our lived experiences and intentionally enact new patterns of thought and behavior. We can engage in lifelong learning until the end of our lives. And we can be generative, supporting younger generations in their projects and aspirations. Goldberg's argument is not based on wishful thinking or unwarranted optimism but on evidence from neurobiology. Researchers today are vigorously investigating wisdom in later life and the meaning of old age; they find a surprisingly positive picture.

Another helpful illustration of this point comes from the idea developed by Psychologist Laura Carstensen, one she has called "**socio–emotional selectivity theory**." She begins with the indisputable fact that, as we get older the time remaining in our life grows shorter. We saw this point confirmed mathematically by Gompertz Law when we looked at the biology of aging. In that respect, it seems that advancing age could bring a confirmation of losses: time is running out. But we have also considered the U-shaped curve of life satisfaction. People grow more satisfied because, with advancing age, they devote more time and attention to activities that support their well-being now, rather than working for goals in the distant future. We typically think of mortality as a "downer." Yet Carstensen's work points to the way in which a shorter time horizon can enable people to focus on what makes them happier. Again, the tendency is not inevitable or universal: we have seen that mental illness is a risk in later life, as it is in earlier stages. But socio–emotional selectivity theory argues that as people get older, they can actually improve at regulating their emotional health.

More than a generation ago, Psychologist Abraham Maslow emphasized the importance of "**self-actualization**," described as a higher level of human functioning, a potential and aspiration of human development that millions of seekers in the 1960s, who were looking for something more in life than conventional material success, found deeply compelling. Like William James a century ago, Maslow called for concerted inquiry into what he called "the farther reaches of human nature." He didn't fill in many of the details, but, decades later, psychology has offered perspectives that can recognize human development as a lifelong process, and that later life and old age hold unique opportunities and gifts. First, there is the emergence of "positive psychology," and the growth of humanistic and later transpersonal psychology, that respond to the challenge Maslow set forth. There are also more recent developments in the context of Gerontology as seen in the Positive Aging movement, and in the areas of humanistic Gerontology and creative aging.

Gene Cohen's *Mature Mind* assures us that the acquisition of wisdom, along with late-life creativity, truly represents one of the "gifts of age" and the gift is not to be understood merely as a continuation of a midlife mentality. Cohen's analysis is much more than the "Don't worry, be happy" message about later-life consciousness. He offers us a detailed analysis of how the mature mind changes and unfolds throughout life. Cohen argues that there are four phases of psychological development in later life: (1) midlife re-evaluation, "a time of exploration and transition"; (2) liberation, an experimental mode which some have termed the "late freedom;" (3) a summing-up phase of "recapitulation, resolution, and review"; and (4) "encore," understood as the desire to go on, perhaps with no obvious limit.

Cohen also defines what he calls "**developmental intelligence**" and claims that these key dimensions of the mind actually improve and expand as we grow into our older selves:

- Relativistic thinking, or a capacity to accept opposing views. Instead of dogmatic truth, we favor a more contextual or relativistic approach to knowledge: "It all depends," as a wise person might say.
- Dualist thinking, where oppositions can be held at the same time in a larger framework.
- Systematic thinking, which permits us to see the "big picture" instead of getting caught up in details.

It is evident that these three dimensions are part of what might colloquially be described as "wisdom." We are used to thinking that wisdom, somehow, is a characteristic goal of old age. Not so with creativity, which we tend to associate with youth. Yet there are many examples of artists who retained great creative power in later life, from Michelangelo among the old masters to Georgia O'Keefe and Picasso in recent times. Gene Cohen has analyzed the "late style" of these aging artists and has discovered in their work many of the dimensions he found in analyzing the mature mind. Mature creativity seems to have much in common with Erikson's idea of ego-integrity and Jung's idea of individuation.

Lars Tornstam's theory of **Gerotranscendence** invites us to look more deeply at those admirable qualities of character found among those who have lived the whole course of life, people who have attained a level of freedom and spiritual fulfillment that can be a goal for us all. Depth Psychologist James Hillman has said that we live in a hyperactive society. Anything less than mania, he quipped, can be considered a possible case of depression. Like Hillman, Tornstam is urging a rather drastic shift in our thinking about what's valuable in life: away from the materialistic in favor of something transcendent or spiritual, even "sitting quietly, doing nothing" (as Zen masters might put it); away from activity in favor of contemplation. Tornstam's message, obviously, will not be acceptable to everyone, certainly not to Gerontologists who subscribe to an "activity" theory of aging (the more the better) or a "continuity" theory of aging (just continue being the self you've always been).

One of the most valuable sources of insight into the psychological gains that might be acquired with aging comes from what is perhaps the longest longitudinal study of human development, the Grant Study at Harvard, which began originally in 1940 and continues to the present. That study has shown that people with strong social ties – to family, friends and community – are in much better shape than people who are isolated or lonely. Those with strong social ties are happier and in better physical health, and these ties seem to buffer people from the inevitable losses and problems of aging, for example, tolerance for pain. Not surprisingly, they also tend to live longer than others. By contrast, those who suffer from loneliness actually show a decline in brain function as well. People who are in a secure positive relationship – where they feel they can count on a partner – are more protected from memory decline. The key to positive social connection is not physical proximity or the number of people but the quality of the relationships. Those with the highest life satisfaction in midlife were likely to be the healthiest in later life. Warm social relationships are highly protective against many declines of later life, according to the findings of more than 75 years of research in the Grant Study.

This description of the aging mind presents a mixed picture. Decline, preservation and improvement are all characteristic of the aging mind. Memory, reaction time and certain information-processing and problem-solving abilities do decline with normal aging. But other cognitive functions remain stable or even improve. Wisdom and experiential knowledge about the ways of the world, for example, are distinctive strengths of older people. Researchers who have examined intelligence testing have concluded that overall physical health and environmental factors, including education, have already made a difference in helping adults preserve cognitive strengths over the life-course. More recently, there has been new attention on training and practice in problem-solving skills, memory techniques, and lifelong learning: all strategies that can help compensate for losses and build on the gains of the aging mind.

RECOMMENDED BOOKS

Erber, J.T. (2013). *Aging and older adulthood*. Wiley-Blackwell: Chichester.

Erikson, E. (1998). *The life cycle completed*. Norton: New York.

Rowe, J., & Kahn, R. (1999). *Successful aging*. Dell: New York.

Stuart-Hamilton, I. (2012). *The psychology of ageing: An introduction*. Jessica Kingsley: London and Philadelphia.

Vaillant, G. (2015). *Triumphs of experience: The men of the Harvard grant study*. Harvard University Press: Cambridge, MA.

Youdin, R. (2016). *Psychology of aging 101*. Springer: New York.

BIBLIOGRAPHY

Social and Demographic Trends Survey from:

Pew Memorial Trust. (2009). *Growing Old in America: Expectations vs. Reality*. http://www.pewsocialtrends.org/2009/06/29/growing-old-in-america-expectations-vs-reality/

From the National Opinion Research Center.

Mroczek, D.K., & Kolarz, C.M. (November 1998). The Effect of Age on Positive and Negative Affect: A Developmental Perspective on Happiness. *Journal of Personality and Social Psychology, 75(5)*, 1333–1349.

McCrae, R.R., & Costa, P.T., Jr. (1987). Validation of the Five-Factor Model of Personality Across Instruments and Observers. *Journal of Personality and Social Psychology, 52(1)*, 81–90.

Rowe, J., & Kahn, R. (1999). *Successful aging*. Dell: New York.

Tornstam, L. (2005). *Gerotranscendence: A developmental theory of positive aging.* Springer: New York.

Cohen, G. (2006). *The mature mind: The positive power of the aging brain.* Basic Books: New York.

Hillman, J. (2000). *The force of character: And the lasting life.* Ballantine: New York.

Cavanaugh, J.C., & Blanchard-Fields, F. (2015). *Adult development and aging* (7th edition). Cengage: Stamford.

Stuart-Hamilton, I. (2012). *The psychology of ageing: An introduction.* Jessica Kingsley Publishers: London and Philadelphia.

Balky, J.K. (1998). *The psychology of aging: Theory, research, and interventions.* Wadsworth Cengage: New York.

Shaie, K.W., & Willis, S. (2015). *Handbook of the psychology of aging* (8th edition). Elsevier Science: New York.

Youdin, R. (2016). *Psychology of aging 101.* Springer: New York.

Heckhausen, J. (1999). *Developmental regulation in adulthood: Age-normative and sociostructural constraints as adaptive challenges.* Cambridge University Press: Cambridge.

Kühn, S., & Lindenberger, U. (2015). "Research on Human Plasticity in Adulthood: A Lifespan Agenda," in K.W. Schaie & S. Willis (Eds.) *Handbook of the Psychology of Aging* (8th edition), Academic Press: Amsterdam.

Australian National Minister Research Group.

4

AGING IN SOCIETY

There is a famous statement attributed to American baseball player Satchel Paige: "How old would you be if you didn't know how old you were?" It's hard for us to take that question seriously because, from the moment we are small children, we are constantly bombarded with feedback about age from others – from parents, from teachers, from playmates. We get messages putting us in a condition where how we're supposed to act depends on how old we are. In school, we take it for granted that we always "know how old we are." We cannot imagine a world different from this. But Satchel Paige's question is worth pondering because it brings our attention to the central topic of this chapter: aging in society.

Pause, reflect, connect: Social aging

How do you go about determining the age or life-course stage of another person in the absence of knowing the year of their birth? What do you pay attention to? What do you consider to be key indicators? Are your perceptions of another person's age or life-course stage accurate?

Let's ask a different question: When do you start to become old? The literature in Gerontology describes that question through the term "age identification." Identifying ourselves as old happens to different people, in different societies, in very different ways. A reader of this book can ask the question in personal terms: When do I feel old? The answer is uncertain: "it depends." For example, if you're in Hollywood (or Silicon Valley) the answer might be "30." The implication is that, above that age, you're "too old." There was a classic self-help book titled *Life Begins at Forty*, first published in 1922, which later was the number one bestseller in the United States. It was an optimistic answer to people who felt they were "too old." For many people studied by Gerontologists like David Karp, it is during their 50s that people begin to "feel old." They start to think about time left to live, rather than just the number invoked by chronological age. The 50s, in Karp's words, are a "decade of reminders" tied to mortality, changes in the body, and other signals, especially messages from others that one had entered a different life-course stage and is no longer "young."

We could also turn the question around and ask "When are you old enough?" Again, the answer is uncertain until we ask "For what?" To buy alcohol, to marry, to drive a car or to vote? Age, clearly, is a qualifying marker for children or young people. In later life, age could also be a qualifying marker: Are you old enough to reside in a senior community, to get a pension, and so on. Gerontologists have used different technical terms in pointing to these questions. For example, they have spoken of "age status" to refer to predictability of qualifying events linked to chronological age. Matilda White Riley spoke of "age stratification," while Leonard Cain spoke of the "life-course," making an analogy of aging to the path of a river. Sociologists remind us that "age" and "aging" are socially constructed concepts and experiences, taking on particular meanings in different times, places and spaces.

Objective standards, linked to chronological age, are easy enough to measure or establish in modern societies. But there remains the domain of subjective standards, either applied to oneself or applied by others, for example, "He's too old for this kind of job," "Is she still driving?" and so on. As applied to oneself, I (Harry) remember a time when I was in my late 60s. As I spoke with a 22-year-old,

I casually mentioned the comedian "Jack Benny," world-famous when I was a child in the 1950s. I took it for granted that everyone knew who Jack Benny was. But I was wrong. That young man had never heard of Jack Benny; Benny was in the same category as Greta Garbo or Rudolf Valentino, I realized. At that moment, all of a sudden I felt "old," conscious that I and the younger person I was speaking with were from very different times.

The two dimensions of objective and subjective age come together in the question: When do people get signals from the world that they are old and begin to believe it? There are many ways to feel old, either suddenly or gradually. Objective and subjective age are tied together. We are not really "only as old as we think" we are, we are also as old as others treat us.

Part of the dilemma in answering these questions is connected to what sociologists call the difference between social structure and **individual agency**. We can cite Satchel Paige again for another statement of his: "Age is a question of mind over matter. If you don't mind, it doesn't matter." Satchel Paige's quip amounts to an assertion of absolute individual agency: you are only as old as you *think* you are. What other people think doesn't matter. This assertion paints individual human beings as possessing choice and action, that is, agency. But in reality, there are also external **social structures** that effect agency: laws, social policies and programs, shared patterns of behavior, expectations by institutions, systems of social stratification, and signals from those in authority. These structures both constrain and enable the sphere of individual agency. When it comes to adult aging and becoming an older person, this distinction between structure and agency becomes incredibly important.

A key take-away message comes down to a simple, but profound, conclusion: aging is not to be equated with the passage of chronological time. We are tempted to believe that aging equals chronological time, but it's not true. For example, even in purely biological terms two 80-year-old people are not "the same age" except when measured by the calendar. One 80-year-old may have had a lifelong accumulation of illness or injury; another 80-year-old could have all the objective markers of superior good health. The one who is sick is more likely to "feel old" than the one who is not. If the chronically ill 80-year-old were to complain, others might say "Well, what do you expect at your age?" This reply is a version of an old geriatric joke, where a patient complains about pain in the right leg. The doctor explains that it's just the result of aging, and the patient replies, "That's funny. My left leg is just as old but doesn't have any pain at all." The physician didn't give a diagnosis but simply repeated a societal expectation, a stereotype, disguised as an explanation. More than a few 80-year-olds will repeat that same societal expectation, having internalized it in what we can call age norms or age expectations.

Another version of societal norms around adult aging comes in the simple 5 letter word "still," as in: "Do you believe it, she's *still* driving!" "He's 85 but he *still* goes to work." We can multiply the examples, but the point is clear: the little word "still" indicates someone who defies age norms or age expectations, perhaps in very positive (but unexpected) ways. It is important to understand that many age norms are actually ageist. Ageist stereotypes, even positive ones, are damaging because they assume that all members of a category are the same, they place strictures on individual agency. Age norms and ageist stereotypes are inside our heads and have been there since childhood. We turn them on ourselves and we project them onto others.

This pattern of age norms and expectations is what we can call the ideology of age. For contemporary societies, that ideology comes down to what social critic Margaret Gullette has called a "decline narrative," that is, a story about how things get worse with age. Robert Butler called this ideology of age by a single term: **ageism**. Butler's key point is that ageism is a form of prejudice – a negative view – about what happens as we grow older. As anti-ageism activist Ashton Applewhite reminds us, aging is inevitable, ageism isn't. Different societies have had very different attitudes toward aging. In traditional Chinese society, for example, old age brought with it a degree of veneration. In Colonial America, elders were given comparable veneration, and British judges traditionally have worn white-haired wigs to underscore higher status. But contemporary Western societies, in Butler's view and Gullette's critique, do tend to hold a negative view of aging and old age. The consequences – such as age discrimination in employment – can be serious indeed.

For further thinking: Aged by culture?

Is aging what happens inside and to the surface of the body or, as Margaret Morganroth Gullette asserts, are we "aged by culture"?

That is, perhaps it is the meaning given to what happens to our bodies as we grow older and how these meanings become embodied and shape our expectations and experiences, that really matter. Gullette suggests that in the context of a youth-oriented society, as is increasingly becoming a global phenomenon as Western consumer capitalism is exported across the planet, growing older and, more significantly, showing one's age, doesn't bring with it greater prestige and authority, especially not in the absence of other positionalities that confer (or don't confer) status. Being old and poor and black and female is a very different experience compared to being old and wealthy and white and male. It is gender, class, race/ethnicity and other positionalities that modify the disadvantaged social status of being old in an ageist social setting. Being old may not in and of itself be a disadvantage – again, the aging experience plays out in individual lives and in the contexts in which they live – as there is no status of "old" that is disconnected or decontextualized from these other positionalities. What's more, where one falls within each of the positionalities in terms of power status also matters.

For example, an older woman may be conferred a great deal of authority and power within her family system because perhaps the ethnic heritage of her family is one that values the contributions older family members make by virtue of their life experiences. However, and in stark contrast, perhaps when she is moving through the social world, going about her daily business, she experiences structural and attitudinal impediments because of how others interpret who she is, based on how she looks on the surface: old, poor, disabled and "ethnic." Sometimes she's treated with unintentional condescension, sometimes she's treated as though she is a mess and needs more help than can be given, and sometimes she's nearly invisible.

THE HISTORICAL MOMENT

Societal influences on aging include both how people feel about themselves and also the impact of social forces that shape age and aging within particular cultural and historical contexts. On this point, Psychologist Erik Erikson famously referred to "life history and the historical circumstance." The point is that the human "life-course" is not like the "life cycle" of insects or other organisms, where the sequence of life stages repeats itself with biological regularity. The human life-course is different. It is profoundly shaped by social forces that come into play in different historical circumstances. We are tempted to think that old age is the same as it's always been – since the Bible or since the Greeks and Romans. But, upon reflection, most of us will recognize that old age is different for today's generation than for our parents or grandparents. "It's not your grandfather's retirement" as some have put it well. We should not think of Gerontology as a science of unchanging regularities and laws. On the contrary, the study of aging is an historical enterprise because aging itself is changing in history, perhaps never so fast as it is today.

To illustrate these ideas, let us consider three different cohorts: the Silent Generation, the Baby Boomers and Generation X. We offer three hypothetical individuals who represent those generations:

- First is Theresa (born in 1937, "Theresa of the Thirties"), born during the Great Depression. Theresa is part of the so-called Silent Generation, the cohort of people born from the mid-1920s to the early 1940s.
- Second is Frank (born in 1957, "Frank of the Fifties"), born at the cusp of the second wave of Baby Boomers (1946–1964).
- Third is Susan (born in 1977, "Susan of the Seventies"), representative of Generation X, born after the time of the post-War Boomers.

There are specific historical events that have had profound and enduring influence on these cohorts, but in very different ways.

We begin with Theresa. The Depression was a decisive influence on the lives of her parents. It is not always true that "Demography is destiny," but demography is important. Fewer children were born during the 1930s, and those lower birth rates would give Theresa a numerical advantage as she grew up. On the other hand, her childhood was likely shadowed by the economic uncertainty of the Depression. If she were a child in London during the Blitz, she

Image 4.1 Aging Over Time

Credit: By Abhikdhar2009 (Own work) [CC BY-SA 3.0 (https://creativecommons.org/licenses/by-sa/3.0)], via Wikimedia Commons.

would likely have been moved to safety outside the City. In any case, she was eight years old when World War II ended, and it remains part of her childhood memories, although in a different way than if she had been born in the US. Frank, too, remembers the veterans of that War, who were in leadership positions throughout society during his childhood.

The economic era of the 1950s provided both Theresa and Frank with a level of comfort and security beyond what was available to children of the Great Depression or World War II. By the 1950s the UK had begun to overcome the shortages of the War and the post-War years. Japan and Germany also had their "economic miracle," which made growing up more comfortable than for those in the Greatest Generation of earlier times. For someone born in the US in 1957, it was a time of golden prosperity, at least if Frank were white and middle-class. That prosperity continued into the 1960s, even as cultural and political turmoil increased.

The decade of "the Sixties" didn't actually begin until the mid-1960s, when ideas of the counter-culture became influential internationally. Theresa is of the same generation as the Beatles. Their record "I Want to Hold Your Hand" was released in 1963, the same year John F. Kennedy was assassinated. Theresa remembers both events vividly, and such marker events have their importance in shaping generational consciousness. But for Frank, a classic Baby Boomer, the bigger impact of "the Sixties" didn't come until he had become a teenager in 1970 and that cultural impact endured into the 1970s.

Theresa came of age and graduated from college in 1958. As a young woman in the 1960s, a period of significant social change, she faced expectations about marriage and employment that belonged to an earlier era. While 1963 was the year that Betty Friedan's *Feminine Mystique* was published, the impact of feminism came much later. The birth control pill did not become widely used until the mid-1960s, spurring changes in sex and gender relationships that Frank, who entered college in 1974, could simply take for granted.

Our last figure, Susan, was born in 1977, three years after a big stock market crash earlier in that decade. The market crash was part of a wider economic decline of the 1970s that was international in scope; the London Stock Exchange fared even worse than the US, losing more than 70 percent of its value. The 1973 oil embargo was repeated in 1979, and the decade was a period of "stagflation." By the time Susan entered school, Ronald Reagan in the US and Margaret Thatcher in the UK had inaugurated a period of conservative reaction in politics. The economic decline of the 1970s was past, and the 1980s and 1990s proved to be a time of economic prosperity, shaping Susan's childhood and adolescence.

The events of September 11, 2001 were vivid for people of all ages, as represented by Theresa, Frank and Susan. Recall our discussion of period effects, large-scale marker events that most people experience and are affected by, regardless of their age cohort membership. Psychologists speak of "flashbulb memories" related to big historic events of this kind. But each one experienced these events at different points in the life-course: 64 (early aging), 44 (midlife), and 24 (young adulthood). Dramatic historical events in themselves need not necessarily influence individual lives, but larger historical trends do have that influence. For example, the coming of the Internet, after 1990, influenced people of all ages, though in different ways. After 1990, Theresa was in her fifties and was not especially keen on learning new technologies. By contrast, for Frank, the aging Boomer, there was no choice but to adapt to the Internet at work and at home and for Susan, as a teenager, surfing the Web became second nature.

Theresa was in the work force from 1960 through 2000, and she was able to enjoy the advantage of a **defined benefit pension** plan, like many others of that Silent Generation. When she retired, even though divorced, she entered the 21st century with a degree of security in retirement. Frank, the prototypical Boomer, turned 50 in the year 2007, a year before the Great Recession, which was a dramatic wake-up call for him as he anticipated retirement not far in the future. He was worried. Susan, who was 31 as the Great Recession began, knew that she still had many years of saving for retirement. She also knew that her previous educational credentials were no guarantee of security in a rapidly changing economy.

Rapid changes in technology and economics have their impact on people of different ages. Facebook was launched in 2005, and by 2008, it had 100 million users, with more still to come. Theresa, aged 71, was initially not on Facebook, but Susan definitely was and it soon became an important part of her social life. By 2017, Theresa had her 80th birthday and was now in the ranks of the "**old-old**." By this time, she had found Facebook valuable for connecting her with old friends and classmates. But in the wider world she often realized that people looked upon her as just an "old lady." In that same year, Frank turned 60 and was not particularly happy in his job but at least was glad to have one. He began to worry about whether his 401(k), a **defined contribution pension** plan, would have enough to support him in later life. Susan, who turned 40 that year, recognized that she was now approaching middle age. Still unmarried, she wondered if it was too late now for her and she also wondered: would age discrimination soon start affecting her?

When we consider Theresa, Frank and Susan at any point in the life-course, we could always ask the question, what does it mean to "Act your age?" For Theresa, who turned 21 in 1958, it might have meant her parents frequently asking her when she would get married. That question would be entirely different for Susan turning 21 in the year 1998, when expectations for women in young adulthood were different. When Frank turned 60 in 2017, expectations about old age had already begun to change: "Seventy is the new Sixty" was a slogan widely heard. But in the labor market, Frank knew well enough that he might now be too old to get a new job if he lost his current one.

The stories of Theresa, Frank and Susan make clear that the sentiment that "You're only as old as you think" is too optimistic and simplistic. This sentiment focuses on individual agency, but not on social structure. The stories of Theresa, Frank and Susan remind us that marriage, educational credentials, the labor market, the stock market, and pension plans are all social structures that profoundly influence how old we feel, how others look on us, and the choices that are available to us as we travel through the life-course. Large historical events, like the cultural upheaval of the Sixties or the Great Recession, will shape and reshape not only individual lives but also the life-course itself.

If Theresa is already in the ranks of the old-old, what will old age be like for Frank, Theresa, and Susan in the future? For example, what will it be like in 2037, when Frank is then Theresa's age in 2017 (80) and for Susan, who will then be 60? By 2037, Theresa, if she lives that long, will be in the ranks of **centenarians**. More than 80 percent of centenarians are female, so her odds are better than Frank on that point. But there are only 17 centenarians for every 100,000 people, so, following Gompertz Law (mortality doubles every eight years), it's very unlikely that Theresa will be around in 2037. But Frank and Susan are likely to be around, and we can wonder what old age will be like for them. As a downside to survival, Frank and Susan could begin to worry about what financial planners call "longevity risk" – that is, running short of money if you live too long.

What old age will be like can't really be known because no one can predict the future, neither in terms of technology, economy, politics nor culture. Did anyone predict the fall of the Soviet Union, the coming of Marriage Equality, or the Great Recession of 2008? But the situation is not hopeless. We can make demographic predictions and note that Frank, an American, is a member of a huge

Baby Boom cohort that is moving through the population like a "pig in a python," to use a metaphor often invoked. The aging of the Boomer generation means that the number of people over 65 will go from 14 percent to nearly 20 percent of the total population.

In 2017 Frank is likely to be worried about Social Security, less than two decades into his future. All analysts on all sides of the political spectrum agree that the US Social Security system will not be able to make full payments after 2034, but instead will have money from the Trust Fund and taxes to cover up to 80 percent of payments promised. So, Frank, anticipating 2037, does have some reason to be worried.

There are other reasons to be worried about the future as well. The current historical period – say, since 2000 – has been an historical time characterized by fear and anxiety. We can point to marker events – September 11, 2001 or the 2008 Great Recession – which inaugurated the dominant mood of the period: loss of control. Ulrich Beck has described this global mood as the "Risk Society." The psychological dimension of vulnerability and risk is disillusionment: the people and social structures we counted on to protect us have failed. People increasingly feel they are "on their own" and cannot count on the social institutions of the past.

The Great Recession of 2008 was not just an aggregate economic shock. In the US, for example, depressed home equity values frightened Boomers away from equity investment. Loss of confidence continued: aging Boomers may rightly have wondered, could the Great Recession happen again? Could it be worse? Who can prevent it? These shocks came on top of long-term decline in defined benefit pension plans and poor saving for retirement. Current period effects also include persistently low interest rates and a legitimation crisis of government credibility. Elections in the year 2016 were only the latest example of it: Brexit in the UK and the election of Donald Trump in the US were a signal of no confidence in political elites.

The period since 2000 has also displayed widening inequality within and across many societies. Aging is part of this picture because aging intensifies other inequalities. The principle of cumulative advantage and disadvantage means that some well-off Boomers have been able to prosper, and join the ranks of the "**Third Age**" (an extended mid-life and postponement of old age) with ample resources. But forces of economic inequality have pushed others into greater risk and vulnerability. Loss of a job or marriage after middle age means, on average, reduced opportunities. Some optimism endures. For example, many aging Boomers tell pollsters they expect to work longer and postpone retirement, which is one solution to diminished pension coverage. But weakness in the labor market, combined with age discrimination and health problems faced by Boomers, make this an option less likely to solve all economic problems for all who enter old age.

Epidemiologists tell us that, as a group, Boomers are in worse overall health than preceding generations of the same age. Despite reduction in cardiovascular disease, aging Boomers face chronic conditions reflecting obesity and poor diet, lack of exercise and mental health problems. Depression and higher suicide rates for older men are part of this picture. Rising divorce rates and more single households come at a time of diminished social capital when more and more of us are "Bowling Alone," to borrow Putnam's phrase (2001). Some studies suggest that loneliness and isolation can have an enormous impact on health outcomes. If the three most important elements for "successful aging" come down to health, wealth and social support, then it appears that aging Boomers are headed for three strikes when they come up to bat in old age. Boomers could be destined to grow old in a period of economic uncertainty, continuing fears of terrorism, and a disaffection with globalization. These trends, which have had an impact on politics in both Europe and the US, will also have an impact on aging in society globally.

RECOMMENDED BOOKS

Applewhite, A. (2016). *This chair rocks: A manifesto against ageism*. Networked Books: New York.

Butler, R.N. (2008). *The longevity revolution: The benefits and challenges of living a long life*. Public Affairs: New York.

Freedman, M. (2012). *The big shift: Navigating the new stage beyond midlife*. Public Affairs: New York.

Gullette, M.M. (2011). *Agewise: Fighting the new ageism in America*. University of Chicago Press: Chicago.

BIBLIOGRAPHY

Karp, D.A. (1988). A Decade of Reminders: Changing Age Consciousness Between Fifty and Sixty Years Old. *The Gerontologist, 28(6)*, 727–738.

Pickard, S. (2016). *Age studies.* Sage: London.

Putnam, R.D. (2001). *Bowling alone: The collapse and revival of American community.* Simon and Schuster: New York.

Thane, P. (Ed.) (2005). *A history of old age.* Oxford University Press: New York.

Tulle, E. (Ed.) (2014). *Old age and agency.* Nova Publishers: New York.

THE POLITICAL ECONOMY
OF AGING

"It was the best of times, it was the worst of times." With these words, Charles Dickens begins his classic novel *A Tale of Two Cities*. We can say the same about old age: for some older people, it is the best of times – people in the so-called **Third Age**, those with leisure, good health, a reliable pension income, and higher life expectancy. For other older people, it can be the worst of times: those who have higher rates of disability, lower life expectancy, and increased rate of poverty in old age. In sum, it is a mistake to think of aging, like death, as the "great equalizer." Later life is a time of inequality, and the political economy of age can help us understand why this is so and what we can do about it, both collectively and as individuals.

The life-course perspective, summarized earlier in the book, is indispensable for appreciating why both heterogeneity and inequality increase in old age. The core of what is happening goes back to what sociologist Robert K. Merton termed the "Matthew Effect," named from a verse in the Gospel of Matthew (25:29), which reads as follows: "For unto every one that hath shall be given, and he shall have abundance: but from him that hath not, even that which he hath shall be taken away." The point here can be reframed crudely as "the rich get richer and the poor get poorer." But the same point applies to health status, social relationships, and many other dimensions of well-being. The point can be generalized and given a name: cumulative advantage and **cumulative disadvantage**.

A good example of this is income inequality based on gender. Women, on average, live longer than men, so we might imagine that this biological difference in life expectancy is the basis of lower income for older women. But that is not the whole story. Women earn less than men earlier in adulthood and women often take time away from work for caregiving responsibilities in the family. Lower wages and time out of the work force earlier in life have a cumulative impact later in life: for example, lower pension accumulations or lower savings. Gender inequality in old age, then, needs to be understood, in part, as the result of inequality earlier in life.

Gerontologists have documented the impact of growing inequality among older people for decades. In the first two decades of the 21st century it has become evident that inequality is growing among individuals and groups in society overall, whether the gap between rich and poor or the gap between wealthy nations and developing countries. Inequality across different countries can even be measured by the so-called Gini coefficient that quantifies the degree to which people have unequal income. Economists and political scientists agree that global inequality is growing more pronounced. But they have different opinions about the causes as well as about the appropriate response to this condition.

Thinking about inequality needs to be connected to the life-course perspective, which treats old age not as a separate stage but as part of an entire life history. Conditions of old age – health, wealth and social position – differ dramatically depending on who one is and their earlier life experiences. Hence, a life-course perspective is imperative for appreciating the widening inequality of circumstances in old age. Along with the life-course perspective, there is the defining demographic trend of the 21st century, namely, **population aging**.

A hundred and fifty years ago, Karl Marx wrote that "A spectre is haunting Europe," namely, the specter of class conflict and proletarian upheaval. Today, in Western Europe, Japan and the US there is a new specter: the fear of an aging society, the gloom that old age is nothing but decline. The French demographer Alfred Sauvy (1976) put it well when he expressed his fear that an aging society would result in a "population of old people ruminating over old ideas in old houses." Fear of an aging society is now an important part of thinking about aging. We will come back to this "gloom-and-doom" attitude toward population aging because it proves to be a critical factor shaping the politics and economics of aging.

At one level, this negative attitude or prejudice could be described as "ageism," the term Robert N. Butler introduced decades ago to describe it. But it also reflects fears about the economic consequences of population aging itself, which often have a very real basis, for example, doubts about the sustainability of public pension programs. On an individual level, ageism and fear of an aging society have never been stronger. For example, so-called "anti-aging medicine" has become a multi-billion-dollar industry, far outpacing the growth of Geriatrics, despite disapproval by mainstream Gerontologists. Many policymakers look at the graying of advanced industrialized societies with dismay but are unable to make changes or offer new solutions, other than cutting the budget or making incremental adjustments in existing programs for an aging population. As with the specter of class conflict when Marx wrote, we now have widespread fear of aging and generational conflict, and this has consequences for politics and economics now and in the future.

POLITICAL ECONOMY

Harold Laswell once famously defined politics as "Who Gets What, When, How." Inquiry into the politics of aging will look at government or policy choices affecting older people – such as taxation, pension programs and healthcare services. These are all concrete examples of "who gets what, when and how." At the same time the politics of aging also considers the political behavior of older voters. Older voters are an increasingly important part of politics today because of the growing proportion of older people in the population and because of the fact that older voters tend to have a higher turnout in elections.

The economics of aging is concerned with the economic wellbeing of older people, for example, accumulation of wealth, income and economic status, employment behavior, and consumption patterns.

In a broader sense, the economics of aging also addresses macro-economic questions, such as savings and investment, which are also related to population aging.

The **political economy of aging** – the approach taken in this chapter – brings together the politics of aging and the economics of aging into a more systemic and unified view. A political economy approach also looks at aging not as a purely individual or biological process – but as the result, at least in part, of larger structures or patterns, for example, social class, gender, race and ethnicity, and education level. A political economy approach is sensitive to the way in which differences, especially forms of inequality, are the result of these larger forces in society. For example, ageism can and does prevent continued employment of older people who want to be in the labor force. And ageism intersects with other forms of discrimination and prejudice such as sexism, classism, ableism and racism. Institutional practices, such as retirement policy and pension eligibility, reflect the interests of organizations such as business or political parties seeking support by older voters. A political economy perspective aims to understand, and critique, collective attitudes and prejudices – such as ageism – as these affect individual behavior and institutional practices.

Two overall principles help us in appreciating a political economy perspective toward aging. First, there is the force of population aging itself, which can be defined as a change in the proportions of young and old: fewer children and more old people. This shift is also reflected in a rise in the average or median age. The trend is illustrated in visual terms by the so-called population pyramid, where children and young people are at the bottom and we move upward to more advanced ages.

As Figure 5.1 vividly illustrates, the 20th century witnessed a dramatic growth in the size of older population globally and in the 21st century we will see the older population grow even more. The proportion of people over the age of 65 (an arbitrary if convenient chronological marker) went from very modest (5 percent or 10 percent) up to very significant in size (15 percent). In the US, by 2030, that proportion will rise to nearly 20 percent. But the trend of population aging in the US is modest compared to what we see in other economically advanced countries. In population

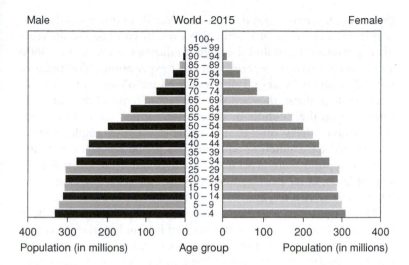

Figure 5.1 Global population aging illustrated

Credit: By English: The Central Intelligence Agency. (The World Factbook.) [Public domain], via Wikimedia Commons.

terms Japan is the oldest country in the world (one-quarter of its population is above 65) and Germany and Italy are not far behind. This demographic trend of population aging has less to do with a rise in life expectancy (modest but significant) than it does with a drop in the birth rate. Declining fertility is the big demographic story, not only in richer countries but also in the developing world. As a result, population aging is the future of global demography overall.

Along with the overall growth of the population age of 65 and older, we need to distinguish the role of specific segments of that population. Thus, those called the "young-old" (65 to 75) will have very different needs and behaviors compared to, say, the "oldest-old" (those over age 85). Along with age effects, we also need to consider differences of generation or **cohort effects**. An individual aged 65 today, for example, is a member of the aging Baby Boomer cohort, while those among the "oldest-old" are part of an earlier cohort, sometimes called the Greatest Generation or the World War II generation. The early years of this cohort were shaped by the impact of the Great Depression and then World War II: in other words, economic and social stress of a distinctive kind. By contrast, the 65-year-old experienced a childhood and youth during the 1950s and 1960s: a time of economic prosperity and great expectations. The point is, not only is the 65-year-old different from the 85-year-old in terms of chronological age, they are also different in terms of the impact of earlier life on their cohort or generation. Finally, we need to consider period effects on aging experiences. For example, today's 85-year-old spent much of adult life in a period when interest rates on bank deposits were favorable to savings. Since the Great Recession of 2008, older people, like everyone else, have lived in a low interest rate environment.

The perspective of political economy tends to promote a deep skepticism about the role of the marketplace and market forces on aging policy. If we accept this critique as a starting point, we are still left with fundamental questions: Must all services for an aging population be provided under government auspice or control? Is there any place for market economies consistent with the critique offered by a political economy framework? How will a growing population of older people influence the economics and politics of aging?

Older people are a growing political force for two reasons: (1) there are more older voters than ever before, because of population aging; and (2) older people as a group turn out to vote more than younger people. For example, in most US elections, turnout by older adult voters has persistently been much higher than by younger voters, especially in off-year (non-Presidential) election years. This fact does not necessarily mean that older people as a group have a "stranglehold" on public policy. But it does mean that the politics of aging looks different today than it did, say, right after World War II, when many European countries adopted social welfare policies, including pension policies, that remain in place today. As population aging increases in Europe, Japan and the United States, we can expect older people to exercise greater influence and we can expect continuing debate about aging policy.

The field of Gerontology has had only a few political scientists who analyze the politics of aging. But the politics of aging will become even more important in years to come because of the aging of the Baby Boom cohort, both in the US and in Europe, as well as trends in global population aging. In a country like Japan, which has demographically the oldest population on earth, elders may make up an important political voice for a different reason. Countries like Germany and Japan, defeated in World War II, have older populations that witnessed an "economic miracle" in those two countries. Today's older population, in their own adult lives, experienced a wave of progress and economic growth not likely to be repeated in the 21st century. The children of today's elders were the people growing up, say, in the 1950s and their political views represent an important cohort effect. Age, period and cohort are all key elements in thinking about the politics of aging.

Immigration is an example of a politically controversial topic where aging is very relevant for two reasons: (1) immigrants, as a group, are younger and therefore, as part of the workforce, they are producers, rather than consumers (making public pensions more sustainable); (2) immigrants, as a group, are likely to be a critical part of the labor force in hospitals and long-term care facilities. In Europe and the US, more and more live in multicultural societies with diverse ethnic groups within the population. The complexion of North American and European cities in the 21st century looks different than it did before. There has been a pronounced negative reaction – fear and worry – among some groups in the population, and older people are among those who are worried the most.

Older people, as a group, have spent their earlier adult lives as workers and contributors to social welfare programs, such as the US Social Security system or public pension programs in European countries. But population aging means that there will be fewer workers, and more pension recipients, than in previous decades. Population aging will put fiscal pressure on those pension programs. In Europe, currently there are 42 pensioners for every 100 workers, but by 2060 that ratio will rise to 65 per 100 workers. In the US, in contrast, there are 24 nonworkers for every 100 who are employed. But both the US and Europe face a parallel problem: in the US, the public pension system, Social Security, will not be able to pay full benefits after 2035. This declining worker-to-beneficiary ratio – called the **dependency ratio** – will be a major flashpoint for political debate in years to come

In the European Union, a common response has been to cut pension benefits, which Greece did after the 2008 fiscal crisis. But the longer-term problem is related to population aging, specifically, declining birth rates, which have fallen by 40 percent since the 1960s. For example, by 2030, 20 percent of Polish men will be 70 or older, while in the US by that year, the population over 65 will be at a similar percentage. When the US faced a Social Security shortfall in 1983, it gradually raised the age of eligibility to 67. Starting in 2012, Poland embarked on a similar gradual rise to age 67, but the political leadership that introduced the change was soon turned out of office. Similar problems are being faced by other countries in the European Union, which by 2017 required national governments to release clear accounting figures of what will be paid to current and future pensioners. On a personal level, many people worry, realistically or not, about what will happen to pension plans, public or private, should we have lagging economic growth or lower prosperity. Many a person asks: Can I count on the pension promises made earlier?

Anyone who has had aging family members or friends has had the experience of watching people of very advanced age (85+) cope with chronic health conditions. Younger adults inevitably ask the question: What will happen to me? A major issue in aging policy in all countries is how to pay for long-term care, whether home-based care or care in a skilled nursing facility. Typically, families are involved in such care, but family members mostly give care to their older members on a volunteer (non-monetized) basis. In countries with strong social welfare provision, the rising demand for long-term care will pose significant fiscal questions: who will pay for it? For countries like the US, with weaker social welfare provisions, a different question arises: how can I save for long-term care?

Long-term care insurance is available in the US, as well as in Germany, Austria, Luxembourg, and other countries. But, in reality, relatively few people buy private long-term care insurance, and, in the US, companies offering such policies have declined dramatically in the 21st century.

There is a prevalent economic discourse that depicts population aging as overwhelmingly a negative development. More and more old people, it is asserted, means fewer people working and more people receiving income through pensions, public or private. This approach typically uses the dependency ratio to define the problem. For example, it is noted that in the US Social Security system, in previous decades there were more people who worked than those who received the public pension. By the early 21st century, the ratio had declined to 3 to 1 and in future decades will decline to 2 to 1. Economists look at the rising number of Baby Boomers who are growing old and forecast unsustainable health care expenditures in the future. Thus, population aging appears as a purely negative development.

But this description misses the complexity of the aging population. A helpful distinction may be between the so-called "Third Age" (the relatively healthy young-old) and the "**Fourth Age**" (e.g., those above 80, who are likely to be more dependent on care). Older people in the Third Age may be retired, but they are not necessarily unproductive. They may spend large amounts of time in volunteering, do-it-yourself activities or informal caregiving within the family. These non-monetized activities are typically not counted when calculating any kind of dependency ratio, and yet they are consequential productive activities. Grouping the Third Age and Fourth Age together tends to reinforce a traditional stereotype of older people as frail and needy and ultimately a drain on society.

Looking at aging from the standpoint of political economy asks us to see the situation of old age not in terms of individual facts – for example, biological or psychological processes – but in terms of the social, political and economic conditions in which people grow old. It asks us, for example, why individuals have such different experiences of old age, where dramatic inequality exists. The challenges and changes that come with growing older are undeniable, as we have seen in looking at the biology and psychology of aging. But a political economy perspective invites us, in the language of C. Wright Mills, to turn "private troubles" into "public issues" shaped by larger economic and political forces.

In a previous chapter, we looked at psychology, the aging mind. The conclusion of that analysis was that changes in the brain – part of the overall biological changes thought to come with growing older – that contribute to changes in the mind can be balanced by selective optimization and compensation: skills of adaptation and resilience.

We might imagine that this is just a matter of individual differences, for example, some people are better than others at coping and adapting. That is true enough. But we should be cautious about interpreting that conclusion in purely individualistic terms. There are patterns that reflect a structure of inequality and political economy. For example, increased life expectancy in the past quarter century has mainly been seen among higher socio-economic levels. In the US, for example, by the early 1970s, a 60-year-old man in the top half of the income level could expect to live a little more than one year longer than a man of the same age in the bottom half. But by 2001, the higher male earner could expect to live nearly six years longer than his counterpart in the lower half. For women, during the same historical time period, the gap was nearly five years longer. Health disparities are closely tied as well to educational levels, which in turn is negatively reflected in obesity, cigarette smoking and cardiovascular disease, itself a key element in dementia.

Consider, too, the case of isolation and role loss in old age, which can lead to depression. We might see those troubles as the natural result of losing one's age-mates to death or because of retirement from employment. But in many societies, older people live in closer proximity to family. Living arrangements like that are much less available in an economy demanding mobility for jobs. In the same way, retirement from employment need not involve complete role loss if there are other roles to make up for the losses. Gradual disengagement might be feasible in an agricultural setting but is less likely when employment and retirement are bureaucratically determined.

Here again is where the political economy framework is illuminating. Contemporary discourse in politics and economy often favors personal responsibility and individual freedom, above all through a free market. Thus, if older persons experience private troubles, maybe they are to blame for their circumstances. For example, if you don't have enough money in retirement, why didn't you just save more? If older people internalize those expectations of individualism, then they may blame themselves for unhappy circumstances in their later years.

The political economy of aging asks us to look at the cumulative results of earlier conditions of life. It is part of what we term the life-course perspective. In the case of income in later life, we could ask why older people, as a group, are less likely to have pension income than older people, say, in 1980. The answer is an historical one. After 1980, changes in the wider political economy caused a dramatic change in private pension coverage by employers. Pensions, when available at all, shifted from a **defined benefit pension**, where employers guaranteed a specific payout, to a **defined contribution pension**, where each individual is responsible for saving and making decisions and investments to assure old age income. This historical trend in practice has meant shifting more risk away from employers and on to individuals who often are unable to save enough or who make poor choices about investment. As well, the political economy perspective asks us always to consider whose interests are being served by particular policies. The shift away from defined benefit plans had beneficial effects on the profits of employers. However, it shifted risk on to employees who often have limited ability to make financial decisions.

A powerful application of a synthesis between the life-course perspective and a political economy view of retirement can be made in considering the current millennial cohort (those born between 1980 and 2000), who face the challenge of saving for retirement. This cohort – larger than the Boomers – in the US, confronts a weak job market, a large student debt load, and housing prices that keep them as renters, rather than accumulating home equity through a home purchase. In Europe, they face high unemployment rates and policies of austerity. In many countries, banks have made lending more difficult. At the same time, many aging Boomers (those born between 1956 and 1964) are still a few years from retirement. They may increase their debt load because they face a declining housing market and low interest rates. These examples of different cohorts underscore why, from a political economy perspective, we need to look at structural factors, such as interest rates, investment returns, home ownership, and employment and pension coverage. Sustainability of public pension systems is certain to be a flashpoint for debate in the political economy of aging for decades to come.

WEALTH AND INCOME

Inequality of wealth (net worth) and income is a striking fact about the older population today. In light of increasing inequality within society, we can expect that inequality in the older population will only increase in years to come.

A lower-wage, hands-on worker can feel "old" at 65, while a skilled and educated professional feels to be in their late middle age. Those with favorable prospects have better health and longevity: they can contemplate lifelong learning or "encore" careers. But for less-educated, lower-earning people, reaching old age means something quite different: lower life expectancy and higher rates of disability. The fact of cumulative advantage and disadvantage means that the chronological "equality" of people the same age – say, 65— is an illusion. Among today's "oldest-old" (85+) those in the top high half of the economic spectrum enjoy 6 years of life longer than those in the bottom half. The gap in life expectancy is expected to grow in years to come.

Because of the Great Recession beginning in 2008 and subsequent financial crises in the EU, many countries in Europe initiated significant reforms in their public pension systems. The reforms were initiated to respond to the need for sustainability of public pensions and also in recognition of issues of intergenerational equity, that is, fairness to different birth cohorts. Austerity policies and economic stagnation in Europe has led to persistently high levels of unemployment for young people.

In the US, traditional or defined benefit pensions were plans where employers made contributions and paid promised benefits. But defined benefit plans have largely been replaced by defined contribution plans, that is, plans where individuals put in savings and depend on performance of investments to assure adequate retirement income. This shift in pension coverage has intensified inequality in old age because defined contribution plans tend to favor wealthier wage earners. Lower-wage workers frequently have no opportunity to participate in any kind of pension plan.

The shift to inequality in retirement income was only intensified by the Great Recession in 2008. Middle-income earners saw a substantial loss in their investments, bigger than higher-income earners. Members of minority groups were at greatest risk and women had other risks because they tend to live longer than men: a report from the National Institute on Retirement Security found that women are 80 percent more likely than their male counterparts to run out of savings in old age. One reason is that women tend to earn less, but another reason is that women, more often than men, take time out of the labor force for childcare or eldercare responsibilities.

Reliance on defined contribution plans has tended to intensify inequality among older people. Inequality must be seen as the result of both political and economic factors. For example, defined contribution plans, such as 401(k) plans, are subsidized by tax exemptions. Such subsidies represent a political decision. The top fifth of earners get around 70 percent from tax subsidies supporting defined contribution plans. The public policy itself intensifies inequality because savings are unequal over the life-course. For instance, those in the top fifth of income are ten times more likely to have a defined benefit plan compared to those in the bottom fifth. In sum, privatization through individual choice tends to make inequality among older persons even more severe.

Europe in recent years has seen a trend toward privatization of pensions that is parallel to recent trends in the US. In European welfare states, there was traditionally more reliance on public pension schemes. But European countries have been moving toward privatization and reliance on free markets. Privatized retirement income in Europe, along with defined contribution plans, tends to make Europe and the US move on parallel paths.

Advocates on behalf of privatization and cuts in public pensions may be justified to the extent that they argue for sustainability of pension programs, for example, state pension programs in the US such as those in Rhode Island or Illinois, among others, where officials promised benefits but failed to contribute enough money to pay for those benefits. But cutting benefits is only one means of insuring sustainability. It is quite possible to raise taxes or contributions to support such programs; such decisions are based on political economy and questions of justice. Advocates of cuts sometimes rely on other arguments, such as urging work–life extension on the grounds that "retirement is bad for your health." But that claim is a legend proved false by 50 years of research. Advocates for cutting benefits may argue that life expectancy has increased so today's older people have dramatically more years in retirement. For example, it is often heard that "Since the early 20th century, we've added at least 30 years to the average life expectancy."

The truth is quite different. Life expectancy, for those who reach age 65, has increased by perhaps 4 years since the mid-20th century. That is an increase, but hardly staggering. It is true that life expectancy at birth increased by 30 years (from 48 to 78) during the 20th century, the greatest gain in human history. But that demographic dividend was largely the result of public health interventions early in life, far less than from any medical breakthroughs enabling us to live longer lives after age 65. A modest gain, yes, but nothing that justifies the claims so often heard. Life expectancy statistics, properly understood, in no way support the argument for cutting retirement benefits.

The challenge of making pension systems sustainable requires long-range thinking and successful resolution of competing political positions. We have seen both success, and failure, in public policy in Europe and the US. For example, in both France and the United Kingdom there have been moves to raise, modestly, the age of eligibility for public pensions, attempts sometimes met with strong public pushback. Other European countries, like Spain and Italy, have faced similar pressures and acted when their retirement systems faced fiscal crisis. In the US, there is agreement that the Social Security system will face a shortfall by 2035, but political paralysis prevents action: those on the right seem to want only cutbacks, those on the left seem to want only tax increases. There is precedence for a reasonable response to this situation. In 1983, the US government acted to make the public pension system sustainable for 50 years, because of effective compromise between opposing political factions. The compromise also involved balancing competing elements of age, period and cohort in order to achieve sustainability.

POSITIVE DIMENSIONS OF AGING

A political economy perspective is indispensable for understanding the condition of older people today. It remains important for the future, when a growing proportion of the population will be above age 60 and the median age will rise in Europe, Japan and the US. But how will we face this major demographic transition?

As we have seen, prevailing public rhetoric tends to depict population aging as a path toward doom and destruction. Younger people in the United States tend to believe that public pensions (Social Security) will be entirely "bankrupt" and not exist in the future, and therefore won't be around to help them in later life. Younger people in European countries suffer higher rates of unemployment while debates rage about whether to keep public pensions intact or reduce them. In many ways, left-wing proponents of political economy ironically end up agreeing with right-wing critics of public pension programs in putting the challenge in purely negative terms, that is, how will we support a growing number of dependent older adults?

Yet economists, looking more carefully into the matter, contradict this gloomy forecast of aging and economic decline. For one thing, older people, even with inequality, have not been the biggest victims of economic problems. For example, a 30-year study by the Brookings Institution found that median real income of working-age families in the US rose around 2 percent (that is, less than one-tenth percent per year), while the median real income of families headed by someone over age 62 rose by more than 40 percent. That is an enormous difference. It does not mean that inequality is not a problem for aging. But it puts that problem in a different perspective.

During the four years after the Great Recession (2007 to 2011) young people between 18 and 25 suffered the greatest income losses, while people over 65 were mostly shielded from the worst effects of the fiscal crisis. Some progressive critics argue that public pension systems have overlooked the rising inequality within the older population. Yet it seems that the biggest risks for poverty have moved from older people to younger people.

The punchline is this: Population aging in itself is not the cause of economic problems. Serious economists have argued that population aging by itself is likely to have only a modest effect on economic growth in the future. A superficial view would lead us to think that a changed age distribution simply means more retired people, and thus a lower level of labor force participation. Yet more careful analysis suggests that the ratio of labor force to population could increase because of lower youth dependency and increased female labor force participation. At the same time, other countervailing factors – such as higher savings for retirement – are already evident since the Great Recession beginning at the end of 2007. Further, there are new pension funding schemes, such as the New Swedish Pension Plan and automatic enrolment plans among various states in the US. Finally, work–life extension and postponing of retirement could encourage more retraining of workers and human capital accumulation on a lifespan basis. All these trends, if seriously encouraged by government policy, could be the basis for sustained economic growth in a period of population aging. There is no reason for gloom–and–doom about longevity and population aging.

Neither political economy nor demography compel us to adopt a gloom–and–doom picture of an aging society. It is entirely possible that we could see a significant shift away from the society we have known in the post-World War II era, a time characterized by early retirement, unsustainable pension promises, and declining investment in the future. All of these tendencies could be reversed in years to come.

When we look at the global picture, we can recognize factors of political economy that could produce a more positive view of population aging. With rising longevity, workers may want to stay in the workforce longer; with the proper incentives – sometimes termed "nudges" workers can increase their savings for retirement and avoid bad choices for investment. Lifelong learning and investment in skills can help older workers remain current and productive. With health promotion and disease prevention, it is possible to reduce dependency in later life.

Some who reject the gloom–and–doom scenario have even argued for a "Golden Age of Aging" in years to come. For example, economists with the World Bank see a future for Europe and Central Asia as a time of healthy, active, and prosperous aging. Instead of economic decline, we could begin to think of a "**longevity dividend**," resulting in the opening-up of new opportunities for an abundance of life. Those pushing the negative image see only a growing burden of chronic disease, hence spiraling expenditures for health and long-term care. They foresee aging societies facing labor shortages and a shortfall in retirement income. But these challenges spring from the fact that current institutional and social arrangements are unsuited for aging populations and shifting demographics. The solution is to change our institutions and social arrangements. The point, again, is that demography is not destiny. To move in this more positive direction, the structures of production and consumption, as well as the politics of aging, must change. A political economy perspective helps us to see how this could happen.

Some of the changes needed, of course, are prompted by the shock of reality, that is, it simply becomes impossible to pay for things already promised and expected. That shock has been one message of the Great Recession. In the US, the shift has resulted in bankruptcy, housing foreclosures, and, significantly, a move away from credit and borrowing in favor of higher personal savings rates. In Europe, the shock has manifested in strikes in Greece and France, where there have been moves to raise the retirement age in order to make pensions sustainable for future generations. These political conflicts are likely to continue. Yet, in both the US and Europe, these painful changes have not yet been matched by a rise in sentiments for solidarity between generations. On the contrary, fear of the future is a sentiment widely felt among many groups, as we have seen in the rise of populist, nationalist and anti-democratic movements in both Europe and the United States.

Part of the problem has been a one-sided focus on production instead of consumption, which overlooks new forms of innovation. Where governments can be paralyzed in acting, business and private non-profit groups are sometimes able to react more quickly to the opportunities for positive aging. Think only of the consumer marketplace. Older people already represent a huge market with significant purchasing power. Consumers over age 50 in the US spend more than $3 trillion each year. By 2017, nearly half the US adult population was 50 years of age or older and they control 70 percent of disposable income, according to Nielsen market research. On a global basis, we see the same trend. Global spending by consumers over 60 could reach $15 trillion before 2020, up from $8 trillion in 2010, according to the Euromonitor research group.

Some of the products bought by older consumers are purely age-related, for example, the infamous "Depends" brand of underwear for incontinence or a medical alert device that beeps when an older person has "fallen and can't get up." The problem with advertising those products is that the message reinforces an ageist image of aging. Equally interesting – and challenging to this ageist construction – is the fact that over 40 percent of products from Apple Inc. are now bought by aging Boomers. Thus, the puzzle: only 15 percent of advertising dollars are spent on the 50+ demographic group, even though they have the greatest discretionary income. Older consumers have been largely ignored by marketers obsessed with youth and suffering from stereotypes that prevent business from seeing opportunities in this huge market segment.

This colossal failure of imagination prevents us from seeing our products and services from the standpoint of our customers. Some of that failure can be traced to internalized and institutionalized ageism and some to a social service mentality: "doing good" for people rather than providing them with services they define in their own terms. From a social service framework, we persist in talking about "needs" while the marketplace moves in another direction, that is, toward aspirations, which is what "successful" aging – and individual agency – is all about.

When we look at the political economy of aging we need to remember that inequality has two sides. Yes, there are impoverished older persons. But there are also sizable groups with money to spend. For example, consider Elderhostel, Inc., which was founded in 1975 and has grown to become the largest education-travel organization in the world. Every year nearly 200,000 older people participate in the program, which is poised for greater growth as aging Boomers are attracted by Elderhostel's new name "Road Scholar." Elderhostel, despite its non-profit status, has operated as a business, constantly innovating and using skilful marketing to reach its customers.

Of the "**Silver Industries**" that promise a new Aging Enterprise of tomorrow, only Elderhostel (Road Scholar) is the most prominent example of an "age brand" among them. Elderhostel operates in the travel and hospitality sector, but there are other sectors also likely to expand in coming decades, for example, healthcare, retirement housing, and financial services. Many innovative activities among Silver Industries provide examples of positive aging in the Third Age.

These Silver Industry sectors will manifest growth driven by a powerful demographic current: every seven seconds, in the US, a Baby Boomer turns 60, which means 10,000 potential new customers each day for the next 18 years. This enormous "age wave" will continue to drive the growth of Silver Industries in years to come, and this growth will represent the leading edge of jobs in the field of

Gerontology. Europe and Japan are even further advanced in this process of population aging. It is a mistake to look at Europe and Japan and believe their aging population is the primary cause of the economic problems they face. Countries with much "younger" populations in the developing world often face far worse economic prospects.

The problem is that if age brands are left entirely to emerging companies in Silver Industry sectors, then we may be in danger of getting products that respond to stereotypes and the lowest common denominator, that is, businesses based on denial of aging rather than latent strengths of later life, such as the field of so-called "anti-aging medicine," which lacks a scientific foundation but appeals to illusory hopes of customers. Many other successful businesses are based on a vision of positive aging. As David Wolfe has shown in *Ageless Marketing*, too many companies approaching the "Mature Market" make huge mistakes and fail to provide the right products and services. Marketers too easily fall into a language distorted by the insidious power of ageism.

Here's the bottom line: The political economy perspective on aging asks us to look realistically at the reality of money and power, economics and politics, all of which influence and shape how older people live and behave. Stereotypes tend to depict older people as uniformly poor and vulnerable. This negative perspective fails to see the emergence of the Third Age and the new opportunities for positive aging. It also fails to recognize the power of Silver Industries and the huge purchasing power of the older population. As pensions have become pre-limited, people approaching old age are likely to think about work–life extension and new forms of **productive aging**. Enlisting the productive power of an aging population will require changes in thought and action for years to come. For example, in the US, and in countries such as Canada and in the UK, mandatory retirement has been made illegal. But mandatory retirement remains legal in most European countries. In virtually all countries, de facto age discrimination prevents employment of older people who want to work and, increasingly, who need to work longer than traditional retirement ages.

The political economy framework invites us to consider the life–course perspective as we recognize how inequality earlier in life – from youth, infancy and even pre-natal conditions – remains an enduring influence on our well-being in later life. The life-course perspective reminds us why older people are not a homogeneous group. Heterogeneity increases with age and so does inequality. This perspective converges with a key element of marketing: segmentation and recognition of differences. A political economy perspective invites us to acknowledge population aging and see the political and economic forces it will bring with it. This dominant demographic trend of our time will continue to influence choices in the marketplace and in the political sphere. The new political economy of longevity could promise solidarity across generations and make possible a long, bright future for our aging society if only we can embrace that future.

RECOMMENDED BOOKS

Carstensen, L. (2009). *A long bright future*. Public Affairs: New York.
Estes, C. (2001). *Social policy and aging: A critical perspective*. Sage: Thousand Oaks, CA.
Hudson, R.B. (Ed.) (2014). *The new politics of old age policy*. Johns Hopkins Univ. Press: Baltimore.
Irving, P. (2014). *The upside of aging: How long life is changing the world of health, work, innovation, policy and purpose*. Wiley: New York.
Vincent, J., & Phillipson, C. (2006). *The futures of old age*. Sage: London.
Walker, A., & Foster, L. (2014). *The political economy of ageing and later life: Critical perspectives*. Elgar: Cheltenham.

BIBLIOGRAPHY

Alslott, A. (2016). *A new deal for old age: Toward a progressive retirement*. Harvard University Press: Cambridge, MA.
Bloom, D.E., Canning, D., & Lubet, A. (Eds.) (Spring, 2015). Special Issue on "Global Population Aging: Facts, Challenges, Solutions and Perspectives." *Daedalus, 144(2)*, 80–92.
Baars, J., Dannefer, D., & Phillipson, C. (2006). *Aging, globalization and inequality: The new critical gerontology*. Baywood: New York.
Bussolo, M., Koettl, J., & Sinnott, E. (2015). *Golden aging: Prospects for healthy, active, and prosperous aging in Europe and Central Asia*. World Bank Publications: Washington, DC.

Carr, D., & Komp, K. (Eds.) (2011). *Gerontology in the era of the third age.* Springer: New York.

Clark, R., Burkhauster, R., Moon, M., Quinn, J., & Smeeding, T. (2004). *The economics of an aging society.* Blackwell: Malden, MA.

Ebbinghaus, B. (2015). "The Privatization and Marketization of Pensions in Europe: A Double Transformation Facing the Crisis." *European Policy Analysis,* pp. 56–73.

Estes, C.L. (2001). *Social policy and aging: A critical perspective.* Sage: Thousand Oaks, CA.

Euromonitor research group. www.euromonitor.com/the-global-later-lifers-market-how-the-over-60s-are-coming-into-their-own/report (accessed January 4, 2018).

Gordon, R.J. (2016). *The rise and fall of American growth.* Princeton University Press: Princeton, NJ.

Hudson, R.B. (Ed.) (2014). *The new politics of old age policy.* Johns Hopkins University Press: Baltimore.

Komp, K. (2011). The Political Economy of the Third Age, in D. Carr & K. Komp (eds.) *Gerontology in the Era of the Third Age,* Springer: New York.

Kunkel, S.R., Brown, J.S., & Whittington, F.J. (Eds.) Springer (2014). *Global aging: Comparative perspectives on aging and the life course.* Springer: New York.

Lynott, R.J., & Lynott, P. (2002). "Critical gerontology." *Encyclopedia of aging.* Gale: New York.

National Institute on Retirement Security, "Shortchanged in Retirement: Continuing Challenges to Women's Financial Future." www.nirsonline.org/index.php?option=content&task=view&id=912 (accessed January 4, 2018)

Piketty, T. (2015). *The economics of inequality.* Belknap Press: Cambridge, MA.

Walker, A., & Foster, L. (2014). *The political economy of ageing and later life: Critical perspectives.* Edward Elgar: Cheltenham.

6

THE MEANING OF OLD AGE

As we reach the end of exploring the basics of Gerontology, we meet what are perhaps the most essential questions of all: What is the meaning of aging and old age? Does aging and old age have any inherent meanings, or is it up to each of us to create those meanings? And, if so, how do we go about creating personal meaning in the last stage of life?

Pause, Reflect, Connect: Age Appreciation

What do you like best about the age you are now?

One way into these questions is a felicitous phrase from essayist Wendell Berry: We live the life we are given, not the life we have planned. Perhaps one of the most important developmental tasks of later life is to reconcile "the life we are given," that is, the life we have actually lived, with "the life we have planned": the hopes, dreams and aspirations for our lives imagined by our younger selves. These questions become ever-more insistent as we grow older. Our past is larger than our future. Plans we had for our future are now replaced by memories of what has been. With the coming of old age, questions about "the meaning of life" are no longer philosophical or hypothetical but pragmatic and concrete, as how we answer these questions shapes our daily lives as older persons.

Gerontology has often avoided questions about "the meaning of old age" in favor of formulations such as "successful aging" or "life satisfaction," as we have seen earlier in the chapter on the aging mind. These formulations lend themselves to measurement by surveys or questionnaires, primary data collection methods used in the social sciences. They give us important insights: for example, the U-shaped curve of happiness, which contradicts prevailing ideas of old age as a gloomy period of the life-course. But this form of research only scratches the surface when it comes to questions about the meaning of aging and old age. Some Gerontologists have probed more deeply: for example, they have used interpretive and narrative approaches, such as ethnography, oral history and autobiography, in order to capture the lived experience of older people. All methodological approaches to researching aging experiences are helpful, and all approaches have limitations. The fundamental point here is that we cannot reduce "the life we are given" – the life we are living – to technique or methodology, or even to what people say in response to inquiries.

The landscape of "old age" is too big for any simple inquiry about its meaning. For example, what happens when individuals move from the (often celebrated) "Third Age" into the (denigrated) "Fourth Age?" What about the duality between the "well-derly" and the "ill-derly," or between those with limited life expectancy (e.g., centenarians) and those who are terminally ill? Is aging a "disease" as some Biogerontologists would argue? Perhaps we should speak about "dis-ease" and suspect that it lies not only in the elders but in the observers, among those of us who are suffering from "hardening of the categories" about the boundary of old age. If we are asked "When does aging begin?" many who have privileged lives are likely to answer "Not yet." Paradoxically, and problematically, Gerontologists are themselves aging at the same time they are objectifying the aging of others.

Questions about the meaning of aging are not new. They go back to ancient civilizations. One of the best examples is the story of

Oedipus, which many of us know in the version that Freud under-stood: the so-called "Oedipus complex." But Freud's version doesn't give the whole story. In the original story, as told by the great Greek playwright Sophocles, we hear of Oedipus as the man who doesn't know his real identity. His parents cast him out as an infant after they heard a prophecy that he would kill his father and marry his mother. Sure enough, as fate would have it, Oedipus ends up being rescued as an abandoned infant, then grows up, meets his real father at a crossroads and, not knowing who he is, kills him in a dispute. Later, Oedipus returns to what was his city of origin where he solves the riddle of the sphinx, which enables him to put an end to the plague affecting the city. He is rewarded by marrying the woman (who is, unknown to him, his real mother) who is the widowed Queen Jocasta.

The key to Oedipus's success comes when he solves the riddle of the sphinx, which goes like this: What creature walks on four legs as an infant, two legs as an adult, and three legs in old age? The answer is, a human being, who in old age relies on three legs, a cane or staff to hold themselves upright. Old age, in other words, is a crucial part of the riddle Oedipus solved, though in a way that still kept him ignorant of his true identity. The playwright Sophocles was obvi-ously preoccupied with the story of Oedipus because he returned to it at the end of his own life, when he was 90 years old, and wrote one of his last plays, Oedipus at Colonnus, a story of what happens to the mythic Oedipus when he reaches old age and achieves a kind of hard-won wisdom.

The myth of Oedipus is far removed from awareness today because it points to the power of fate. When Wendell Berry refers to "the life we are given" in contrast to the life we have planned, Berry is pointing to this contrast between what we think of as our choice and the life we were fated to live. But we only begin to real-ize this later in life, and that insight may be a crucial part of the meaning of adult aging and old age. In the riddle of the Sphinx the image of "walking on three legs" is an allegory of the Fourth Age: disability, decrepitude, erasing of those strengths of midlife that we celebrate and through which we define ourselves. Yet we, like Oedipus, cannot grasp the true riddle of our existence, the meaning of our lives, until we have lived, not the life we have planned, but the life we have been given, including all the stages of life, most especially the last stages.

Our public discourse, including the discourse of Gerontology, is very far from thinking deeply about the meaning of aging and old age. In fact, that public discourse, which insists on choice and autonomy, can impoverish our understanding of the last stage of life. We too easily accept the prevailing liberal presumption that "meaning" is something individual and private. You have your version of meaning and I have mine, and that's the end of the story. But making the public–private duality into a wall of separation promotes a fatal forgetting of history, of conditions that affect us all, though in different ways. In previous chapters, we saw that what we call the life-course is actually shaped by sociocultural and historical forces in multiple ways. There are no private values, any more than there are private languages. But once banished to the night-world of privatism, meaning becomes invisible in the dark.

"I don't feel old" is a spoken version of privatism. The cheerful bromide "You're only as old as you think" is another such version. Both responses reflect the unexamined assumption that feelings are detached from social connection or that individuals can invent themselves and be any age they want. "I don't feel old" and "You're only as old as you think you are" ignores the epidemic of ageism in our time. We imagine that ageism is merely "discrimination against older people." True, we saw in the preceding chapter how prevalent ageism remains. But the deepest form of discrimination is more subtle and insidious. The deepest form is internalized discrimination, discrimination of older-people-against-themselves, as well as younger persons' fears and anxieties about their own future older selves. It is ironic that ageism is abundantly evident in societies which, in demographic terms, are vanguards of "population aging," such as Japan and Europe. Aging is all around us, but it is "hidden in plain sight" – aging is everywhere and nowhere at the same time – because we do not look at it, do not listen to the voices of elders, including the voices of our future older selves. By making adult aging more visible, by reaching out across generational differences, we can challenge and perhaps dismantle ageism.

In an earlier chapter, we discussed so-called Silver Industries, which often depend on a very positive image of old age as a time of retirement, fulfillment and happiness. The meaning of old age, in this version of the life-course, is a time of tranquillity and relief from burden: life on the golf course or playing shuffleboard, on one level, or traveling the world through Road Scholar, on another. This idea of meaning in later life is depicted very well in the last of four paintings, the "Voyage of Life" painted by the 19th-century American artist Thomas Cole.

Cole offers a highly romanticized picture of old age. The previous paintings in the series "The Voyage of Life" show a hero traveling by boat down the river of life, moving from infancy, to youth, to turbulent midlife. Old age, as depicted by Cole, is a time of rest: the river has gone in the calm ocean, while an angelic guide comes to offer transition to the afterlife. For contemporary older persons, this "afterlife" might well be the period of retirement itself, if considered in a positive light. If much of adult life is stressful, retirement can be imagined, romantically, as a time of freedom and fulfillment – a time of "positive aging."

But what could positive aging signify in terms of the meaning of old age? At a minimum, we might say that meaning in life is the opposite of depression, or a feeling that life is not worth living, that it is worthless. Richard Leider has focused on the idea of purpose in life, which could be described as having a reason to get out of bed in the morning. In a broader sense, Leider has described positive aging as "life reimagined," emphasizing the need for people to redefine their purpose as they grow older. Here, let us take the idea of purpose and purposeful living as a starting point for meaning in old age. Let us explore positive aging through three ideas about meaning in later life: successful aging, productive aging, and conscious aging.

SUCCESSFUL AGING

Let us recall that in Rowe and Kahn's definition, it is not defined by external circumstances, such as wealth or health. Those who identify their sense of "meaning" with these attributes may find disappointment in old age and even become depressed. But successful aging can also be defined as "decrement with compensation," which involves resilience and adaptation to change and challenge. We recall that, in the riddle of the sphinx, elders walked on three legs, with a cane. But they still walked, which implies a degree of activity and positive meaning in life.

Ancient thinkers – Sophocles as well as Cicero and the stoic philosophers – understood that our control of fate, or what happens to us, is very limited. But we do retain a degree of control over our attitude toward things that happen to us. Jan Baars describes this perspective as the "art of living" and argues that in contemporary society, where old age may be devalued and disregarded, elders still retain the ability to adopt a positive attitude toward their lives and circumstances. In other words, to find meaning in life – to experience successful aging – does not require freedom of action, which is likely to be constricted in advanced age. It requires instead a change in our consciousness. Baars relies on Nietzsche, Heidegger and existential philosophers to emphasize the importance of freedom in choosing how we think of meaning in our lives. Meaning is not a given, but must be created, much as we create a work of art. Mary Catherine Bateson (*Composing a Life*) offers a similar perspective in which an individual life is composed, much as a piece of music would be. This point is close to what was expressed by concentration camp survivor Viktor Frankl (*Man's Search for Meaning*), who said "Everything can be taken from a man but one thing: the last of human freedoms – to choose one's attitude in any given set of circumstances, to choose one's own way." If we think of the search for meaning in old age as "decrement with compensation" then Frankl's affirmation is the ultimate compensation that promises meaning in later life.

Finding meaning in old age has a parallel with what Psychologist Carl Jung called "individuation" or finding your true self apart from roles or social requirements. The feeling was well summed up by the painter Matisse in his old age when he said "It's bothered me all my life that I don't paint like everyone else." Matisse, in old age, was crippled and confined to a wheelchair. Like the aged Renoir, Matisse could barely hold a paintbrush so he shifted his artistic practice to producing pieces of colored paper and cardboard: the famous "woodcuts" that comprise his supreme achievement in old age. Matisse, though severely physically limited, was nonetheless able to pursue the path of "decrement with compensation" and express a radical sense of meaning of individual integrity. Successful aging, in all its manifold forms, is a way of seeing life as a work of art and finding meaning in old age.

PRODUCTIVE AGING

Another approach to meaning in old age is well expressed by the phrase "the need to be needed." Productive aging is a version of positive aging, which emphasizes that, while growing older, people can continue to make contributions to their communities and to society at large. This idea that to be productive is the way to find meaning in old age is captured well by existential philosopher Simone de Beauvoir:

> The greatest good fortune, greater even than health, for the old person is to have his world still inhabited by projects: then, busy and useful, he escapes both from boredom and decay. The times in which he lives then remain his own, and he is not compelled to adopt the defensive and aggressive forms of behavior that are so often characteristic of the final years. His oldness passes as it were unnoticed. For this to be the case he must have committed himself to undertakings that set time at defiance.
>
> (1996, pp. 492–493)

De Beauvoir argues that a strategy of productive aging is ultimately the way to find meaning in old age: "There is only one solution if old age is not to be an absurd parody of our former life, and that is to go on pursuing ends that give our existence a meaning" (1996, p. 540).

Nancy Morrow-Howell and her colleagues have shown that productive aging is a powerful and important direction for today's older people to find meaning in old age. The challenge is to find ways in which older people can channel their interests and talents into productive activities: for example, through work–life extension in "encore careers," or through volunteerism, or through contributive activities among family, friends and neighbors. The idea of productive aging has a large resonance in the contemporary world because it promises us a way to make later life into something affirmative: a form of "positive aging." Of course, that promise will only be fulfilled if physical and psychological strength continues to a degree, and if social opportunities exist so that people can contribute to the needs of others around them.

CONSCIOUS AGING

At the age of 82, Florida Scott-Maxwell, a playwright and psychotherapist, began to keep a journal recording her feelings about growing older. The result was the book *The Measure of My Days*, which begins with these stirring words: "We who are old know that age is more than a disability. It is an intense and varied experience, almost beyond our capacity at times . . ." (2000, p. 5). Her approach, then, is to find meaning in old age by discovering what is special and distinctive about it. This approach is what we can call conscious aging; namely, the turning inward and, to some degree, turning away from the things that gave meaning to us earlier in life. Thus, successful aging (optimal health, activity, connection with others) and productive aging (the need to be needed, contributive roles) are not at all what interests Florida Scott-Maxwell.

Her approach is captured well in these lines from her journal:

> Age puzzles me. I thought it was a quiet time. My seventies were interesting, and fairly serene, but my eighties are passionate. I grow more intense as I age. To my own surprise I burst out with hot conviction. Only a few years ago I enjoyed my tranquility; now I am so disturbed by the outer world and by human quality in general that I want to put things right, as though I still owed a debt to life. I must calm down. I am far too frail to indulge in moral fervor.
>
> (pp. 13–14)

Scott-Maxwell's idea of owing a "debt to life" has something in common with Simone de Beauvoir's assertion that meaning in old age is found in a deep connection with the wider world. But to fulfill this "debt to life" demands a degree in inner-directedness that might not have been possible in earlier phases of the life-course. The paradox is that advanced old age, the "Fourth Age," is likely to be a time when the condition of one's body makes it more difficult to act in the wider world. We should note that Scott-Maxwell died at the age of 90 and completed her journal while living in a nursing home. But her limitations do not in any way diminish her search for meaning. She speaks of the "fierce energy" or passion that she feels, a passion that her limitations make it impossible to be put into action: "If I try to transpose it into action I am soon spent. It has to be accepted as passionate life, perhaps the life I never lived, never guessed I had in me to live." The meaning of old age, for Scott-Maxwell, is to be found not in activity but in the intensity of consciousness itself: "it may be a degree of consciousness which lies outside activity, and which when young we are too busy to experience" (pp. 32–33).

What is interesting about Florida Scott-Maxwell is that she is offering an idea of meaning in old age that draws on what is distinctive about advanced age, what is less possible earlier in life. Her perspective here makes us realize that many forms of "positive aging" are actually ways of insisting that we don't have to grow old at all, but can maintain the same sources of meaning that are found earlier in life. "Success" and "productivity," after all, are widely heralded values. Countless people find meaning in later life by continuing to support the values and activities that inspired them in youth or middle age, preserving these as long as possible. These habits, to which we give the name of success and productivity, are limited by the inevitable losses of later life: bereavement and greater vulnerability of the body. Above all, they are limited by the changing sense of time: we have more time behind us than ahead of us.

One of the major points we come to as we ponder the meaning of old age reminds us of the contradictions that can often be experienced in the last stage of life. Because of the prejudice of ageism and the disengagement of retirement, older people may lose a clear sense of the identity they worked to establish over the previous stages of the life-course. Along with this loss may come a degree of freedom, that is, the ability to be one's "true self," independent of what others think. When we read the writings of authors who speak from personal experience about aging, what is striking is the great diversity and individuality of responses. To find meaning in later life seems to be something each of us must find for ourselves and in our own way. The idea of "meaning," then, is not to be equated with Robert Browning's optimistic poetry about age: "Grow old along with me,

The best is yet to be." Many, like Simone de Beauvoir, would reject Browning as purely sentimental. That leaves us with a question about the meaning of old age: how do we find a way to be realistic, avoiding denial, while at the same time remaining hopeful?

When Erikson wrote about the last stage of life, we remember, he framed it as a juxtaposition between "ego-integrity" and "despair." That pairing suggests that both could have their place in the meaning of old age. Loss, in other words, is not to be avoided but faced up to: loss of age-mates through bereavement, loss of physical strength, loss of time ahead of us, and, ultimately, the loss of our life when we reach our end.

Here, again, we are in the presence of a paradox. In the Fourth Age, physical limitations easily become apparent, but, as Florida Scott-Maxwell says in her journal, that can lead to a more acute sense of appreciation of the world around us. That contradiction is nowhere more visible than in the self-portraits made by the great Dutch painter Rembrandt. Rembrandt made his self-portrait more often than any artist in history: fully ten percent of all his works are self-portraits.

Rembrandt died at the age of 63, hardly what we would describe as "old age" today. His life was marked by great losses: he lost his beloved wife Saskia, his career as an artist went into decline, and he had to face bankruptcy and foreclosure of his house and the loss of all his possessions. In one of his last self-portraits, we see Rembrandt bent over, as if crushed by the weight of years and sorrows. The painting, like others he did in his last years, was rendered with very rough brushwork, in the manner we have come to recognize as the late style of some aging artists. Rembrandt looks directly at us, the viewers, and he is smiling, as if laughing in the face of all the losses in later life. The painting brings together all of the contradictions we find as we search for the meaning of age both in our own lives and in our wider society. It was the great art critic Ananda Coomaraswamy who said, "It's not that the artist is a special kind of person. It's that each person is a special kind of artist." Perhaps there is no greater challenge than to see our lives as a channel of creativity: in becoming a "special kind of person" we become the person we were meant to be, even in – perhaps especially in – the last years of life.

RECOMMENDED BOOKS

Bateson, M.C. (2001). *Composing a life*. Grove: New York.

Booth, W.C. (Ed.) (1996). *The art of growing older: Writers on living and aging*. University of Chicago Press: Chicago.

Leider, R., & Webber, A. (2013). *Life reimagined: Discovering your new life possibilities*. Berrett-Koehler: San Francisco.

Lustbader, W. (1991). *Counting on kindness: The dilemmas of dependency*. Free Press: New York.

Schachter-Shalomi, Z., & Miller, R. (1995). *From age-ing to sage-ing*. Time Warner: New York.

BIBLIOGRAPHY

Baars, J. (2012). *Aging and the art of living*. Johns Hopkins University Press: Baltimore.

Cole, T.R. (1992). *The journey of life: A cultural history of aging in America*. Cambridge University Press: New York.

de Beauvoir, S. (1996). *The coming of age*. W.W. Norton: New York and London.

Morrow-Howell, N., Hinterlong, J., & Sherraden, M. (Eds.) (2001). *Productive aging: Concepts and challenges*. Johns Hopkins University Press: Baltimore.

Rowe, J., & Kahn, R. (1999). *Successful aging*. Dell: New York.

Scott-Maxwell, F. (2000). *The measure of my days*. Penguin: New York.

7

EPILOGUE

How does Gerontology cohere as an academic discipline and field of practice when increasingly other disciplines and fields are taking on issues of aging, old age and later life? What constitutes Gerontology's purview or territory when aging is everywhere (we are all doing it) and nowhere (there are so many mixed messages and they all seem to be about others' experiences, not our own) at the same time? As well, not only are academic disciplines and fields outside of Gerontology taking on the questions, issues and problems that have traditionally been the focus of Gerontology, but there has been a proliferation of niche services, products, businesses and marketing strategies targeted at older populations (but often with little or no grounding in gerontological knowledge). The good news: no matter what path you may follow in terms of education, career and lifelong learning, you will have ample opportunities to be in contact with, even serve, older persons, as there isn't any area in society that doesn't touch on, to some degree, issues of aging, later life and old age.

When questions about aging, old age and later life are relevant to such a wide variety of knowledge workers and practitioners, we might wonder about the relevance and sustainability of Gerontology. What makes Gerontology different than, say, psychology or sociology?

Image 7.1 Grandmother Hands
Credit: Photograph taken by author, Jennifer R. Sasser.

A better question might be: How does the work of a Gerontologist differ from the work of a Psychologist or sociologists who focus on aging issues? Is there something special about Gerontology as a field and a Gerontologist as a particular kind of knowledge worker and practitioner? Are there issues, questions and problems over which Gerontologists have exclusive purview? And how are the boundaries between Gerontology and other fields of study and practice regulated (and by whom?). We ask again: how would you know a Gerontologist when you saw one? We might also want to ask some critical questions about the relevance of Gerontology – or any other discipline or field of practice. To what extent are Gerontologists – in their many guises, individually and collectively – intentionally reflecting upon where their field came from, how it is constituted contemporaneously, and where it might need to go in the future in order to fulfill its promise? This question seems particularly relevant given the global explosion in population aging, the Baby Boom cohort's entrance into later life, and the many complex issues connected to individual longevity and societal aging. Perhaps as we move ever farther into the 21st century there will be a special purpose served by some Gerontologists who commit to following the work being done inside as well as outside the field, with the aim of integrating perspectives and knowledge across the various domains in which research and practice around adult aging issues is happening.

As we approach the end of this book, we feel it bears repeating that human beings are multidimensional creatures who are not only biological organisms but makers of meaning in complex contexts – minds, spirits, social actors, members of societies and cultures, and travelers through time. As such, to understand, let alone explain, the adult aging process (which, as we've hopefully demonstrated, is actually multiple interconnected and complex processes), we need to explore every facet of the human experience. This requires the individual and collective efforts of many researchers, theorists, practitioners and teachers working both within the field of Gerontology – in all of its many varied forms – as well as without in allied and other disciplines and fields. Interestingly, the work produced by scholars and practitioners working from outside of the disciplinary boundaries of Gerontology often provides valuable perspectives for considering the phenomena that fall under the purview of Gerontology. In my (Jenny's) own experience – first as a student and then as a professional working in the field of educational Gerontology – some of the freshest and most impactful ideas that have influenced my work I discovered beyond the walls of Gerontology. Given the complexity of the phenomena upon which Gerontology focuses, and given that the lived experience of aging is a multifaceted, contextual and emergent process, it almost goes without saying that there's room for – even the necessity for – theoretical perspectives and empirical insights that come from not only disciplines allied to Gerontology, but even those that may seem initially to have little to offer inquiry and practice focused on adult aging and later life. As well, alongside the burgeoning scientific research on the multifaceted aspects of adult aging, we should encourage the generation of perspectives on the aging experience and old age that are best created through the arts and humanities. There are exciting intellectual and creative currents inside and outside the field of Gerontology that are challenging the dominant construction of adult aging and mainstream scientific approach to its study: cultural Gerontology; humanistic Gerontology; critical Gerontology; narrative Gerontology; and aging studies.

We urge that the questions we've been asking throughout this book about Gerontology as a field, and the nature of multifaceted adult aging phenomena at the center of gerontological inquiry and practice, are questions not only relevant for Gerontologists to be asking, but are questions that may have personal relevance for you, the reader, as well. Aging isn't something happening to other persons, it is a process we are all experiencing, and not at some time in the future, but now. We don't suddenly become an old person, rather, we are engaged in the long unfolding of growing older. The question is: do we want to engage in our own aging process, in our travels through the life-course, with some measure of intentionality and awareness? Do we want to be keen in knowing about the ways in which knowledge about adult aging is constructed (and the implications of this knowledge for how aging adults are treated)?

Perhaps this is where our true agency resides as we travel into the farthest reaches of the life-course, even in the face of the enormous changes and challenges that come with aging in adulthood, that is, in our capacity to greet our future older selves and engage as fully as possible with our aging as a process intertwined with our living.

For further exploring: Befriending our future older selves

How about inviting your future older self for a visit? How about if the two of you were to become friends? Here are some questions to contemplate:

- When you visualize your future older self, who and what do you see?
- How much older are you than you are at present?
- How far into deep old age are you able to travel in your imagination?
- When you imagine your future older self, how do you feel? What sensations do you experience in your body? What thoughts do you think?
- When you imagine your future older self, where are you? What are your surroundings and where do you live?
- What are your hopes for your future older self? (And what are your fears?)
- How will you live fully in your older body, in whatever state your older body happens to be?

- How will you use fully your older mind, in whatever state your older mind happens to be?
- What are some of the ways you will experience enjoyment, freedom and passion with your aging body?
- Who are the other creatures in your life? With whom will you spend time and enjoy life?
- What do you feel is your purpose as an old person?
- What new things is your future older self learning and experiencing?
- What does your future older self consider to be a "good day"?
- What changes in your thinking and acting do you need to make in your current life in order to have the old age you envision?
- What does your future older self want to tell your present self?
- If you invited your future older self over for a cup of tea or a glass of wine, what would the two of you talk about?

GLOSSARY

Activities of Daily Living ("ADLs"): Personal care activities such as bathing, dressing, toileting and moving around.

Adult aging: The normal, multifaceted processes of aging that begin at maturation and continue until the end of life.

Age-associated: Patterns in any of the dimensions of human aging (body, mind, social world, etc.) that are associated with increasing age but not caused by aging processes in and of themselves.

Age identification: As people move through the life-course, how they perceive themselves as having entered later life and the social status of being an old person.

Ageism: As originated by Butler, the concept of prejudice and discrimination regarding age and aging.

Aging effects: Changes thought to be caused by the physiological processes of aging, as well as the meanings of those changes in various sociocultural contexts.

Amyloid Hypothesis: The hypothesis that plaques and tangles in the brain of Alzheimer's patients show a distinctive deposition of the amyloid protein.

Antagonistic pleiotropy: The theory that certain genetically determined traits could be beneficial for survival early in life but become harmful at later ages.

Apoptosis: When a cell self-destructs, or "commits suicide," according to a programmed instruction.

Between-group differences: In cross-sectional studies, differences between age groups being compared on some measurement, e.g., performance on a memory test for a group of college age subjects compared to a group of older adult subjects.

Bio-markers: Specific biophysical and functional processes thought to change because of increasing age in adulthood.

Bio-psycho-social approach: As part of the Life-course Perspective, emphasizes that aging is not only a biophysical process, but a multifaceted process involving body, mind, social contexts.

Caloric restriction: Reduction in the amount of daily calorie intake, a process which has evidently slowed the rate of aging in invertebrates, birds and mammals.

Causation: A change in a dependent variable is caused by an independent variable.

Centenarian: A person 100 years of age and older.

Cerebral vascular dysfunction: Small strokes that damage brain tissue over time.

Chronological age: The number of years one has been alive since birth.

Classic aging pattern: In intelligence testing, the consistent pattern of relative stability or even increases in verbal scores but declines in performance scores with increasing age.

Cohort: A group of people born within a bounded period of years.

Cohort effects/differences: The influence of experiences members of an age cohort/generation share because of when they were born.

Compression of morbidity: As proposed by Dr. James F. Fries, the idea that people could remain healthy up until the last month or year of life, then die rapidly of natural causes.

Continuities and discontinuities: In life-course research, the patterns over time in individuals' abilities, attitudes, behaviors and capacities. The extent to which these factors change or stay the same as individuals mature and grow older.

Correlation: The direction and strength of the relationship between variables.

Cross-sectional research: A methodological design in which groups of people of different ages are compared at one point in time.

Cross-sequential design: A research design that simultaneously considers age effects, period effects, and cohort effects while examining differences and similarities *between* age cohorts, and change and stability over time for individuals.

Crystallized intelligence: As measured on an intelligence test, the intellectual capacity to use experience as the basis for solving problems or completing tasks.

Cumulative disadvantage: The negative and intensifying impact of early life events on an individual's experiences in subsequent phases of the life-course.

Decrement with compensation: The concept that as adults age, optimal functioning requires acknowledging and adapting to losses.

Defined benefit pension: Pension program whereby employers guarantee employees a specific payout.

Defined contribution pension: Pension program where each individual is responsible for saving and making decisions and investments to assure old age income.

Dementia: A set of organic neurological and cognitive diseases, the most common of which is Alzheimer's Disease.

Dependency Ratio: A measure of the economic burden on the working population caused by those not in the labor force.

Dependent variable: In experimental and quasi-experimental research design, the variable hypothesized to be influenced in a causal or correlational way by different levels of the independent variable.

Developmental intelligence: Cohen's assertion that key dimensions of the mind improve and expand with adult aging.

Epigenetics: Variations in cellular behavior and physiological traits that come about because of environmental forces that switch on (or off) the genes in our cells.

Executive function: Overall cognitive control, attention span, and control of behavior.

Extrinsic: Factors influencing aging which originate from outside the organism.

Five-Factor Model: Of personality: Costa and McCrae have identified neuroticism, extraversion, openness to experience, agreeableness, and conscientiousness as the five factors of personality.

Fluid intelligence: As measured on an intelligence test, the intellectual ability to solve novel tasks and problems.

Fourth Age: Refers to persons older than 80 years of age, who are likely to experience chronic health issues and frailty.

Frailty: Assaults or damage of any kind to the body. Declining reserve capacity of biological systems.

Free radicals: Atoms with unpaired electrons that are very reactive. Free radicals are formed in many chemical reactions, including those in normal metabolism.

Functional age: A definition of age different from chronological age which is based on an assessment of how individuals function in daily life, such as regarding Activities of Daily Living or cognitive capacity.

Gains and losses: Adult aging can be described as a balance between gains and losses in each of the domains in which aging occurs.

Geriatrics: The medical speciality that focuses on the diseases and disabilities associated with aging and later life, as well as the health and long-term care needs of older adults.

Gerontologist: There are many and varied descriptions of a "Gerontologist." In general, these are persons who have received special education and training and work in the field of aging. A Gerontologist may work in healthcare, social services, education, business, research or policy, focusing on some aspect of adult aging and later life issues.

Gerotranscendence: Tornstam's theory of late-life development describing a rather drastic shift in our thinking about what's valuable in life: away from the materialistic in favor of something transcendent or spiritual.

Glycosylation: Among the most universal of all chemical changes in living things are those involving sugar (glucose). Like oxygen, glucose is fundamental for metabolism. And may also be fundamental to biological aging.

Gompertz Law: The statistical pattern whereby death rates double with every 8 years of increasing age.

Habituation: Kastenbaum's assertion that as humans grow older they become habituated in response to the environment, a process that may begin early in life and intensify over time.

Hayflick limit: The maximum number of cell divisions that normal cells undergo in the lifetime of an organism.

Health span: Rather than the number of years lived, e.g. lifespan, this is a concept that captures the quality of the extra year lived with longevity.

Heterogeneity in aging: Differences between individuals increase with increasing age. Individuals become less alike the older they grow.

Idiographic: Theoretical explanations for, or empirical measure of, phenomena occurring at the individual level of analysis.

Independent variable: In experimental and quasi-experimental research design, the variable hypothesized to exert a correlational or causal influence on the dependent variable.

Individual Agency: The extent to which an individual can exercise choice and control over their lives.

Individuation: The idea that an imperative of adult development is to become fully and uniquely oneself.

Interdisciplinary: Different perspectives from multiple disciplines are combined or integrated: the sum is greater than its parts.

Inter-individual differences: Differences between individuals within a group, such as in cross-sectional research comparing two or more age groups.

Intrinsic aging: Normal biological aging processes that originate from within the organism.

Later life: The last segment of the adult life-course.

Learned helplessness: An individual's experience of dependency and depression resulting from social and physical environments that reinforce lack of agency and passivity.

Life-course: The stages and phases through which human beings pass over the course of their lives, from infancy to old age.

Life-course perspective: A theoretical perspective that views multifaceted aging processes as unfolding over the entire human life-course in a series of interconnected states, from birth to old age.

Life expectancy: A population-level measurement predicting the average length of life; can be measured from birth or any age, such as the average length of life for persons 65+.

Lifespan: A hypothetical maximum length of life for any species.

Lipofuscin: A kind of "debris" that accumulates in cells with aging that may interfere with cell function over the course of aging.

Locus of control: An individual's subjective perception of their ability to influence their environment and manage their daily life.

Longevity dividend: The positive benefits of increasing longevity resulting in the opening-up of new opportunities for an abundance of life.

Longitudinal research: A methodological design in which the same group of research subjects is followed over time.

Multidisciplinary: Multiple perspectives that come from different disciplines – psychology, sociology, political economy, medicine, etc., are utilized in a complementary and additive way.

Nomothetic: Theoretical explanations for, or empirical measure of, phenomena occurring at a generalizable level of analysis.

Normal aging: Also, referred to as "senescence." The biophysical changes that are thought to occur to some extent for all human beings and which result in increased vulnerability and decreased resistance to disease.

Old age: Often used interchangeably with "later life," *old age* is the social and existential status of being an old person. The chronological marker for when old age begins varies across societies and cultures.

Old-old: The functional age group composed of adults ages 75–84.

Oldest-old: The functional age group composed of adults 85 years of age and older.

Osteoporosis: The loss of bone mass and density associated with advancing age.

Paradox of aging: Older adults subjectively perceive and report their health status to be stable even when they are experiencing chronic health issues.

Period effects: Large-scale events of issues that affect people of all ages and generations living in society at the same time.

Plasticity: The capacity even into advanced older age for improvements in cognitive, mental and physical functioning through learning new skills and abilities.

Political economy of aging: The approach that brings together the politics of aging and the economics of aging into a more systemic and unified view, considering aging not as a purely individual or biological process but as the result, at least in part, of larger structures or patterns.

Population aging: Results in an increase in the average age of a population; may also involve an increase in the proportion of a population that is composed of older persons.

Productive aging: The idea that while growing older, people can continue to make contributions to their communities and to society at large.

Reserve capacity: The capacity of a human body to recover from illness and injury, as well as to withstand peak-load demands on its organ systems.

Sarcopenia: Degeneration of muscle mass and loss of both strength and quality. Not caused by age but associated with increasing age.

Selective optimization with compensation: Older people who are aging "successfully" may gradually narrow the scope of the capabilities they seek to maintain to those who are most useful and important.

Self-actualization: Described as a higher level of human functioning, a potential and aspiration of lifelong human development.

Senescence: Normal biophysical changes resulting from adult aging processes.

Silver Industries: Services and business that target the needs and aspirations of older adults.

Social determinants of health: How individuals' aging experiences are strongly influenced by who they are, where they live, and their access to social and economic resources and capital across the entire life-course.

Social structures: Often presented in an antimony with "individual agency," the structures and institutions in a societal system which both enable and constrain the exercise of individual agency.

Socially constructed meanings: The idea that individual meanings of, expectations about and behaviors related to, age and aging are shaped by social structures and discourses, rather than being universal and essential.

Socio-emotional selectivity theory: Carstensen's theory that with adult aging a shorter time horizon can enable people to focus on what makes them happier.

Successful aging: As defined by Rowe and Kahn, the optimal combination of good physical and mental health, high quality social connections, and a sense of meaning and purpose in life.

Telomeres: The "caps" on the tips of chromosomes. In each cycle of cell division, telomeres get shorter.

Third Age: Older adults experiencing an extension of the aspirations of midlife. Those with leisure, good health, reliable pension income and higher life expectancy.

Vital capacity: The maximum amount of air that can be breathed in and out by the lungs.

Young-old: The functional age group composed of adults ages 65–74.

INDEX